INSIDE

LANGUAGE · LITERACY · CONTENT

Acknowledgments

Grateful acknowledgment is given to the authors, artists, photographers, museums, publishers, and agents for permission to reprint copyrighted material. Every effort has been made to secure the appropriate permission. If any omissions have been made or if corrections are required, please contact the Publisher.

Photographic Credits

Cover ©JH Pete Carmichael/Riser/Getty Images. **Back cover** ©Loeiza JACQ/Gamma-Rapho via Getty Images. **1** ©Jupiterimages/BananaStock/Alamy. **3** ©Image Source Black/Alamy. **4** ©Tony Freeman/PhotoEdit. **5** ©Ian Shaw/Alamy. **6** ©UpperCut Images/Alamy. **9** ©Jose Luis Pelaez, Inc./Blend Images/Corbis. **11** (tl) ©Jeff Greenberg/PhotoEdit. **11** (tr) ©MM Productions/Corbis. **11** (bl) ©Simon Jarratt/Corbis. **11** (br) ©Dana White/PhotoEdit. **14** ©Janine Wiedel Photolibrary/Alamy. **45** (t) ©Matt Henry Gunther/Taxi Japan/Getty Images. **45** (b) ©PhotoAlto/Alamy. **46** ©CorbisRF/Alamy. **59** ©David Young-Wolff/PhotoEdit. **95** (bkgd) ©The Stocktrec Corp/BrandX/Jupiter. **95** (c) ©DLILLC/Corbis. **101** ©NASA/Handout/Getty Images. **102** ©Ray Massey/Photographer's Choice/Getty Images. **198** ©Foodfolio/Alamy. **214** ©Foodfolio/Alamy.

For product information and technology assistance, contact us at **Cengage Learning Customer & Sales Support, 888-915-3276**

For permission to use material from this text or product, submit all requests online at **www.cengage.com/permissions** Further permissions questions can be emailed to **permissionrequest@cengage.com**

National Geographic Learning | Cengage Learning
1 Lower Ragsdale Drive
Building 1, Suite 200
Monterey, CA 93940

Cengage Learning is a leading provider of customized learning solutions with office locations around the globe, including Singapore, the United Kingdom, Australia, Mexico, Brazil, and Japan. Locate your local office at **www.cengage.com/global**.

Visit National Geographic Learning online at **ngl.cengage.com**
Visit our corporate website at **www.cengage.com**

ISBN: 978-12854-39044 (Writer's Workout)
ISBN: 978-12854-39075 (Writer's Workout Teacher's Annotated Edition)

ISBN: 978-12857-68007 (Writer's Workout Practice Masters)
Teachers are authorized to reproduce the practice masters in this book in limited quantity and solely for use in their own classrooms.

Contents

Table of Contents, continued

Table of Contents, continued

Editing and Proofreading Marks

Mark	Meaning	Example
∧	Insert something.	The first time I met Dawn was ∧at the swimming pool.
∧	Add a comma.	"I know I can trust you in this∧" I said.
∧	Add a semicolon.	Dawn is a great friend∧she comforts me when I feel low.
⊙	Add a period.	I am glad Mr⊙Pendleton didn't get mad at us.
⊙	Add a colon.	Dawn practices many sports⊙basketball, soccer, swimming.
∨ ∨	Add quotation marks.	∨Could I speak to you for a moment?∨ I asked.
∨	Add an apostrophe.	Dawn∨s cat is called Barn Daddy.
≡	Capitalize.	I go to Rosa Parks middle school.
/	Make lowercase.	Dawn and I decided to talk during our /unch break.
℘	Delete; take something out.	I also showed her the notes for my report.
¶	Make new paragraph.	"I need your help with my report," I said.¶"I am afraid I won't have time for this today," she said.
⬭	Check spelling.	We (studyed) for more than 5 hours.
∧̄	Replace with this.	All that studying really ∧affected my grades.
∼	Change order of letters or words.	I like Dawn because she is always reli∼able.
#	Insert space.	We spend #alot of time together.
⌒	Close up; no space here.	Dawn and her family live in a farm⌒house.

Analyze a Paragraph

What makes this paragraph a good model?
Read the paragraph and answer the questions.

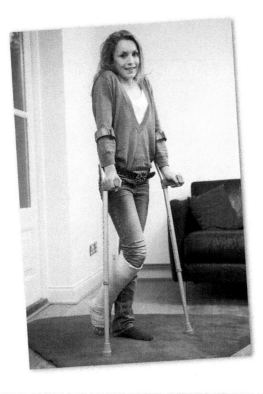

Making the Best of It

by Savannah Tavares

When bad things happen, people should try to look for the positive side of the situation. For example, last summer I broke my leg. Since I wasn't able to play outside much, I decided to take a summer-school course. In class, I learned how to use sign language. I spent a lot of time studying and did well in the course. Now, I volunteer as a translator for deaf individuals in my community. If I had never broken my leg that summer, I would not have learned this helpful skill. It just goes to show that you can always make the best out of a bad situation.

Feature Checklist

A good paragraph

☐ has a topic sentence that states the main idea

☐ contains details that tell more about the main idea.

---

1. Does this paragraph have a topic sentence?

_____
_____
_____
_____
_____

2. What main idea is stated in the topic sentence?

_____
_____
_____
_____
_____
_____

3. How do the paragraph's details tell more about the main idea?

_____
_____
_____
_____
_____
_____

State a Topic Sentence

Study each writing topic, main idea, and details. Once you see how the details fit with the topic, write a good topic sentence for each example.

1.

Topic: Learning a new language
Main Idea: Its many benefits
Details:
- cultural education
- can communicate with more people
- helps you integrate into a new culture

Topic Sentence:

2.

Topic: Learning a new language
Main Idea: Difficulties
Details:
- hard to learn new words
- pronouncing new sounds is difficult
- new grammar rules to remember

Topic Sentence:

3.

Topic: Learning a new language
Main Idea: Ways to learn
Details:
- computer programs
- classes
- travel

Topic Sentence:

Analyze a Problem-and-Solution Paragraph

What makes this problem-and-solution paragraph a good model? Read the paragraph and answer the questions.

A Great Idea
by Meeshak Smith

I had a lot of trouble thinking of a topic for my social studies essay. It was due on Monday, and I thought I could come up with something during the week. I knew I should ask someone for help, but I didn't want to look dumb. By Friday, I still didn't have any ideas. Finally, I decided to ask someone for help. I went to my friend Ezra because he's great at coming up with ideas. When I told Ezra how much trouble I was having, he offered to help me on Saturday. We went through my notes together and talked about what had interested me the most in class. Soon, I had a topic picked out and was able to start my essay. I worked all day and was able to finish my work by Saturday night. I'm so glad I decided to ask Ezra for help. If I hadn't, I might still be trying to come up with a topic!

Feature Checklist

A good problem-and-solution paragraph

☐ presents a problem

☐ explains the problem clearly and in detail

☐ presents a solution

☐ explains how the solution addresses the problem.

1. **What problem is presented in the topic sentence?**

   _____

   _____

   _____

   _____

   _____

2. **What solution did the writer arrive at?**

   _____

   _____

   _____

   _____

   _____

   _____

   _____

3. **What are some details that the writer gives about the solution?**

   _____

   _____

   _____

   _____

   _____

   _____

Analyze a
Chronological-Order Paragraph

What makes this chronological-order paragraph a good model? Read the paragraph and answer the questions.

Feature Checklist

A good chronological-order paragraph

☐ tells events in the order they happened

☐ uses words like *first, next, then, after,* and *finally* to show the sequence of events.

1. What does the topic sentence tell you about the paragraph?

_____

_____

_____

_____

_____

_____

Ryan's Fall
by Carlos Contes

When Ryan and I decided to go for a bike ride on Sunday, we didn't expect anything unusual to happen. At first, it was a perfectly normal bike ride. But then, Ryan hit a bump, and the next thing I saw was him falling. After he hit the ground, I ran over to him and asked if he was all right. Then I knocked on my neighbor's door and told her what had happened. She came outside and brought ice for Ryan's knee. After that, she told me to stay with him while she called for help. Soon, an ambulance came and the paramedics looked at Ryan's knee for a while. Finally, they took Ryan to the hospital, where he found out that he would be fine.

2. What is the first event Carlos tells about?

_____

_____

_____

_____

_____

_____

3. What signal words and phrases does the writer use to transition between events?

_____

_____

_____

_____

_____

_____

© National Geographic Learning, a part of Cengage Learning, Inc.

Analyze a Spatial-Order Paragraph

What makes this spatial-order paragraph a good model? Read the paragraph and answer the questions.

Melissa's Room
by Kendra Brown

Everything Melissa decided to put in her room reflects her personality. Before you enter the room, you'll find a door covered with posters of paintings by her favorite artist. When you walk in and look to your right, you'll see a closet door covered in more art. The art there isn't by a famous artist—it's by Melissa. The wall next to it is a work of art as well. She's decorated it with a giant collage of photos of her friends. Over on the other side of the room you'll see framed awards that Melissa received for her artwork. Her bed is alongside that wall. A colorful quilt that Melissa herself made covers the bed. The wall at the farthest end of her room has a huge window. Melissa glued small pieces of colorful tissue paper on top of the glass to make it look like a stained-glass window. Every inch of the room shows that Melissa is an artist.

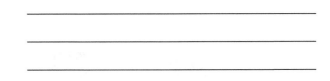

Feature Checklist

A good spatial-order paragraph

☐ proceeds from a visual starting point to an ending point

☐ takes the reader logically from one place to the other

☐ uses signal words like *over* and *beyond* to show spatial order.

1. **What is the starting point of the spatial description?**

_____

_____

_____

_____

2. **What kind of spatial order does the writer use?**

_____

_____

_____

_____

3. **What signal words and phrases does the writer use to show where things are?**

_____

_____

_____

_____

Analyze a Compare-and-Contrast Paragraph

What makes this compare-and-contrast paragraph a good model? Read the paragraph and answer the questions.

Stephen and I

by Carter Stone

My best friend Stephen and I are similar in some ways and different in others. Stephen has lived on our street all his life. In contrast, I have moved six times in my life and have lived here only for about a year. But we are alike in so many ways that we became friends quickly. Both of us are big music fans, so we are always introducing each other to our favorite songs. Stephen used to listen only to classic rock. However, I like a lot of newer music, and I've convinced him to listen to some of it. I also like classic rock, so we have some of the same favorite songs. My music is what gets me through long bus trips. Similarly, Stephen won't leave home without something to listen to. We have lots of other things in common, of course, but music is one of the most important things to both of us.

1. **What two things does the author compare? Are these things alike, different, or both?**

   _____

   _____

   _____

   _____

   _____

2. **How are the two similar? How are they different?**

   _____

   _____

   _____

   _____

   _____

3. **What signal words does the writer use to make comparisons and contrasts?**

   _____

   _____

   _____

   _____

   _____

Plan and Write a Paragraph

Use pages 7–8 to plan and write a paragraph on a topic related to your life.

1. Decide what you want to write about. List ideas about your topic. Circle the most important idea you want your readers to understand.

_____

_____

_____

_____

_____

2. Now list details and examples that support your main idea.

_____

_____

_____

_____

3. Choose an organization method and write a topic sentence for your paragraph. Sketch and fill in a graphic organizer to help you structure your paragraph.

Topic Sentence: _____

_____

4. Now follow your plan from page 7 to write your paragraph.

Name _____ Date _____

Collect Ideas

Check out the idea file on pages 9–10 and add some ideas of your own.

Photos

Memories can inspire you to write.

Quotations

"Each indecision brings its own delays and days are lost lamenting over lost days. . . What you can do or think you can do, begin it. For boldness has magic, power, and genius in it."

— Johann Wolfgang von Goethe

"Nothing is more difficult, and therefore more precious, than to be able to decide."

— Napoleon Bonaparte

_____
_____
_____
_____
_____
_____

© National Geographic Learning, a part of Cengage Learning, Inc.

Topics That Interest Me

1. The day I decided to join the basketball team

2. When I volunteered at the shelter

3. The time I asked for help in math

Collect Ideas, continued

Speak Your Truth

Write a "truth" for each photograph. Tell what the photograph suggests is true about people or about the world.

1.

_____

_____

_____

_____

2.

_____

_____

_____

_____

3.

_____

_____

_____

_____

4.

_____

_____

_____

_____

Choose Your Topic

1. Use the graphic organizer to help you narrow down your topic. Make your topic specific enough to cover in a couple of pages.

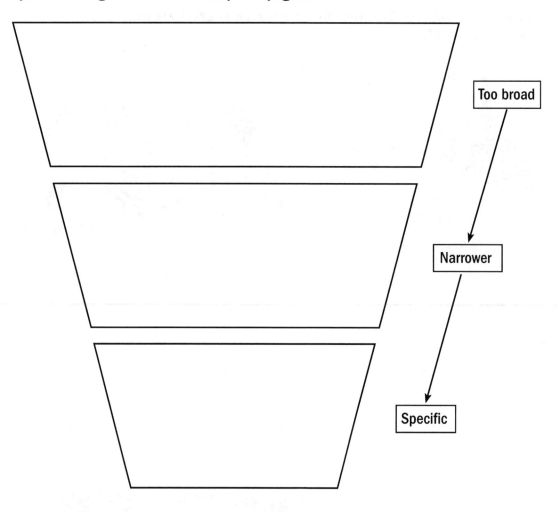

2. What, specifically, are you going to write about? Describe how you plan to approach the topic.

_____

_____

_____

_____

_____

_____

_____

_____

_____

_____

Write for Different Audiences

1. Complete the chart. Write the tone and give an example of the language that should be used for each audience.

Audience	Tone	Language
your best friend or someone your age	very informal	Hey, Laura. Are you going to the costume party tomorrow night?
an older relative		
your teacher		
someone you don't know		

2. Circle the number that shows how often you write for each audience.

How often do you write for . . .	Never	Rarely	Sometimes	Often
❶ yourself?	1	2	3	4
❷ friends?	1	2	3	4
❸ family?	1	2	3	4
❹ teachers?	1	2	3	4
❺ employers?	1	2	3	4
❻ strangers?	1	2	3	4
❼ someone else: _____?	1	2	3	4

3. For whom do you most like to write? _____

Write for Different Purposes

1. **Study the chart. Add examples from your own writing or reading experience for each purpose listed.**

If You Want Your Audience to. . .	Your purpose is. . .	Your form is. . .
· learn something new · understand something better	to inform or explain	*directions*
· laugh · feel deep emotion · enjoy reading your work	to narrate	
· believe something · do something · know how you think or feel	to argue	

2. **Study the photo. Choose two different purposes from the chart above. Write a few sentences about the photo for each purpose you chose.**

Purpose 1: _____

Sentences: _____

_____

_____

Purpose 2: _____

Sentences: _____

_____

_____

Organize Your Ideas

Study the writer's FATP chart and notes. Then organize the information in different ways.

FATP Chart

Form: *personal narrative*

Audience: *classmates*

Topic: *my family's move to a new town*

Purpose: *to explain why I'm happy we moved*

Notes About the Topic

- *Last month, my family bought the house next door to my friend Jamie's house.*
- *Now Jamie and I hang out in my family's new yard almost every day.*

- *I used to live far away from all my friends.*
- *The school is down the street, so in the fall, Jamie and I will walk to school together.*

1. Read the topic sentence. Organize the notes in logical order.

Topic sentence: *I'm glad my family moved because now I get to spend more time with my best friend, Jamie.*

Details:

2. Use the graphic organizer to write the notes in chronological order.

3. What event from your life will you write about for your personal narrative?
Complete the FATP chart. Then choose a graphic organizer that goes with
your purpose and form. Complete the graphic organizer to help you organize
your ideas.

FATP Chart

Form: *personal narrative* _____

Audience: _____

Topic: _____

_____

Purpose: _____

_____

Draft Your Personal Narrative

Use your plan from page 16 to write the first draft of your personal narrative.

Drafting Checklist

- ☐ Tell a true story, with a beginning, middle, and end.
- ☐ Make sure the order of events is clear.
- ☐ Use specific details to help the reader "see" what happened.
- ☐ Express your thoughts and feelings about the event.
- ☐ Keep the style and tone appropriate for the intended audience.

Get Ready to Revise

Evaluate the Writing

The writer of the passage below plans to read her work aloud at a conference on friendship that will be attended by students as well as adults. Her purpose is to narrate a personal experience about friendship. Read the paper aloud to yourself. Consider the audience and purpose, as well as other aspects of the writing. Make notes on feedback you would give to the writer of this paragraph.

My Best Friend

From the first day we met in elementary school, Courtney and I have been inseparable, more like sisters than friends. Even our moms are great friends. Courtney has avoided hanging out with me. She confessed to me that her mom got a new job, so her family was moving, and she felt terrible. When I confronted her about the situation, her face got red, and she started to cry. She gave me her favorite necklace, so I wouldn't forget her. It's a silver elephant with a pink jewel in its eye. It's my favorite necklace. I think of her whenever I put it on.

My Feedback to the Writer

_____

_____

_____

_____

_____

_____

_____

_____

_____

Gather Ideas

Use this page to think about your writing, get feedback, and plan what changes you'll make to your paper.

1. Read your paper to yourself. What parts sound good to you? What parts need more work? Why? _____

_____

_____

_____

2. Read your paper aloud to one peer and one adult. Ask them how you can improve your draft. Write down any answers you can use to revise your paper.

_____

_____

_____

_____

_____

3. Have a peer conference. Use the feedback you get to answer these questions:

What's the best thing about your writing?

_____

_____

What do you need to work on to improve your writing?

_____

_____

What other changes did your readers suggest?

_____

_____

4. Now you're ready to decide how you will revise your paper. Describe the changes you plan to make.

_____

_____

_____

Revise: Mark Your Changes

1. Use the checklist to evaluate this draft of a personal narrative. What changes are needed?

_____

_____

_____

_____

_____

2. Revise this draft. Use revising marks to show your changes.

Revising

MARK	WHAT IT MEANS
∧	Insert something.
↶	Move to here.
∧—	Replace with this.
ℓ	Take out.
¶	Make a new paragraph.

My Best Friend

From the first day we met in elementary school, Courtney and I have been inseparable, more like sisters than friends. Even our moms are great friends. Courtney has avoided hanging out with me. She confessed to me that her mom got a new job, so her family was moving, and she felt terrible. When I confronted her about the situation, her face got red, and she started to cry. She gave me her favorite necklace, so I wouldn't forget her. It's a silver elephant with a pink jewel in its eye. It's my favorite necklace. I think of her whenever I put it on.

3. Now use the checklist and your notes from page 20 to help you revise the draft of your personal narrative on pages 17–18.

Edit and Proofread

Tools: The Dictionary

Edit the passage below. Use the dictionary excerpt at the bottom of this page.

> I could not sleep, thinking that I might have cheated on my report.
>
> I decided I had to conferr with someone I trusted. I thought my cousin
>
> Lydia would make a great person to confyde in. In fact, she had been
>
> my confydent for a long time. Lydia confermed my fears and told me
>
> to confess. She said that maybe I would be confinned to my room for a
>
> long time, but that it was the right thing to do.

confer • confound   190

con•fer (kuhn-fur), *v.* **-ferred, -fer•rin.** —*v.i.* **1.** to discuss something together; compare opinions. —*v.t.* **2.** to give as a gift, honor, etc.: *to confer a prize.* —**con•fer'ra•ble**, *adj.* —**con•fe'rral, con•fer'ment,** *n.* —**con•fer'er**, *n.*

con•fer•ee or **con•fer•ree** (kon-fuh-ree), *n.* **1.** a person on whom something is conferred. **2.** a person who participates in a conference.

con•fer•ence (kon-fer-uhns, -fruhns), *n., v.,* **-enced, -enc•ing.** —*n.* **1.** a meeting for discussion: *a conference between a teacher and a parent.* –*v.i.* **2.** to participate in or hold a conference.

con•fer•ence call, *n.* a telephone call that connects three or more people at the same time.

con•fess (kuhn-fes), *v.t.* **1.** to acknowledge and reveal a fault, crime, or weakness. **2.** to admit as true. **3.** to admit one's sin to God or to a priest. —**con•fess'able**, *adj.* —**con•fess'ing•ly**, *adv.*

con•fes•sion (kuhn-fesh-uhn), *n.* **1.** acknowledgment; admission. **2.** something that is confessed. **3.** formal and written admission of guilt in a crime. **4.** acknowledgement of one's sin to God or to a priest.

con•fes•sion•al (kuhn-fesh-uh-nl), *n.* **1.** based on confession. **2.** part of the church devoted to confession.

con•fes•sor (kuhn-fes-er), *n.* **1.** a person who confesses. **2.** priest who hears confession.

con•fet•ti (kuhn-fet-ee), *n.* **1.** small bits of paper, thrown during a celebration or a festive event. **2.** candies; bonbons.

con•fi•dant (kon-fi-dant), *n.* **1.** a person to whom secrets are confided.

con•fi•dante (kon-fi-dant), *n.* **1.** a woman to whom secrets are confided.

con•fide (kuhn-fahyd), *v.* **-fid•ed, -fid•ing** —*v.i.* **1.** to tell someone about a secret or a private matter. **2.** to trust someone or something completely. **3.** to entrust. —**con•fid'er**, *n.*

con•fine (kuhn-fahyn), *v.,* **-fined, -fin•ing.** *n.* —*v.t.* **1.** to limit or restrict: *I confined my remarks to the latest events.* **2.** to shut or keep in; to keep someone or something within certain limits of space: *My father confined me to my room for the rest of the evening.* —*n.* **3.** boundary; limit; border. —**confined**, *adj.*

con•fine•ment (kuhn-fahyn-muhnt), *n.,* **1.** the act of confining **2.** the state of being confined.

con•firm (kuhn-furm), **1.** to establish as correct; verify: *She confirmed my doubts.* **2.** to make definite. **3.** to strengthen someone's opinion or habit. —**confirmed**, *adj.* —**con•firm'able**, *adj.* —**con•firm'a•bil'i•ty**, *n.* —**con•firm'er**, *n.*

con•fir•ma•tion (kon-fer-mey-shuhn), *n.* **1.** the act of confirming. **2.** a piece of evidence.

con•fis•cate (kon-fuh-skeyt), *v.* **-cat•ed, -cat•ing**, *adj.* —*v.t.* **1.** to seize with authority. **2.** to take something as a punishment. —*adj.* **3.** seized. —**con'fis•cat'a•ble**, *adj.* —**con'fis•ca'tion**, *n.* —**con'fis•ca'tor**, *n.*

con•fla•gra•tion (kon-fluh-grey-shuhn), *n.* an extensive and destructive fire. —**con'fla•gra'tive**, *adj.*

con•flate (kuhn-fleyt), *v.t.,* **-flat•ed, -flat•ing.** *n.* to merge; fuse together. —**conflation**, *n.*

con•flict (*v.* kuhn-flikt; *n.* kon-flikt), *v.,* **-flict•ed, -flict•ing**, *n.* —*v.i.* **1.** to clash; disagree. **2.** to fight; do battle. —*n.* **3.** disagreement; quarrel. **4.** strong opposition. —**conflicting**, *adj.*

con'flict of in'terest, *n.* the circumstance in which a public officeholder has personal interests that interfere with his or her office's responsibilities or duties.

con•flu•ence (kon-floo-uhns), *n.* **1.** flowing together of two or more rivers or streams. **2.** point of junction of two or more rivers or streams. **3.** the act of coming together of people or things.

con•flu•ent (kon-floo-uhnt), *adj.* **1.** merging into one; flowing together: *confluent ideas; confluent rivers.*

Edit and Proofread, continued

Tools: Personal Checklist

Use page 23 to create your own personalized checklist of mistakes to watch out for.

1. Look back through your old papers to see which editing and proofreading errors are marked most frequently. Jot down your top five trouble spots.

_____

_____

_____

_____

_____

2. Talk with your teacher about ways to fix these mistakes, or check out a style handbook for tips.

3. Now, create your personal checklist. List your most common mistakes and explain how you can fix them.

☐ Words I mix up:
- "they're" and "their"

  "They're" is a contraction. Try substituting "they are" in the sentence to see if it still makes sense.

Using Editing and Proofreading Marks

Edit and proofread this passage. See how many grammar, spelling, punctuation, and capitalization errors you can find. Fix the errors using the marks on page 25.

The Tricky Part

Proofreading my on work can be tricky. Since Im familiar with my own essay, I have a tendency to read through it to quickly. This can led to missing some major msitakes.

Their are lots of places that mistakes can hide. Finding there location can be easy fi you know where to look. For example I no that I some times missuse the words *there* and *their*. So I read threw my essay one line a at time and make sure I am using those words correctly. I also know I tend to transpose letters when type. I read my essay backword to to look for those mistakes.

I usually to like have a friend proofread my essay. A fresh pear of eyes can help find mistakes I may have missed. I usually ask my friend jessica. When she reads my essay she takes her time and looks it over carefuly. Mosttimes we trade papers, and I will Proofread her essay as well If I knotice that Jessica has made the same mistake multiple times, I make a not. When I'm finished, I tell her "you occasionally forget to add a period at at the end of you sentences You might want to add that to your personnel checklist.

Edit and Proofread, continued

Editing and Proofreading Marks

Mark	Meaning	Example
∧	Insert something.	The first time I met Dawn was ^at the swimming pool.
∧	Add a comma.	"I know I can trust you in this ∧" I said.
∧	Add a semicolon.	Dawn is a great friend ∧ she comforts me when I feel low.
⊙	Add a period.	I am glad Ms ⊙ Pendleton didn't get mad at us.
⊙	Add a colon.	Dawn practices many sports ⊙ basketball, soccer, swimming.
ᵛᵛ ᵛᵛ	Add quotation marks.	ᵛᵛ Could I speak to you for a moment? ᵛᵛ I asked.
ᵛ	Add an apostrophe.	Dawn ᵛ s cat is called Barn Daddy.
≡	Capitalize.	I go to Rosa Parks ≡ middle ≡ school.
/	Make lowercase.	Dawn and I decided to talk during our /lunch break.
℘	Delete; take something out.	I ~~also~~ showed her the notes for my report.
¶	Make new paragraph.	"I need your help with my report," I said. ¶ "I am afraid I won't have time for this today," she said.
⬭	Check spelling.	We (studyed) for more than 5 hours.
⌃‾	Replace with this.	All that studying really ᵃ∧ effected my grades.
∼	Change order of letters or words.	I like Dawn because she is always reli(ab)le.
#	Insert space.	We spend a #lot of time together.
◡	Close up; no space here.	Dawn and her family live in a farm ◡ house.

Editing and Proofreading in Action

Grammar Workout: Check for Correct Sentences

Add a subject or predicate to each incomplete sentence, to make it complete. If you add a predicate, make sure the verb agrees with the subject.

1. Carlos's cousin _____ .

2. _____ hopes to become an NBA player one day.

3. Leo's coach _____ .

4. _____ met Leo, thanks to Carlos.

5. Leo _____ .

6. _____ can make a lot of money.

7. The biggest stars of the game _____ .

8. _____ spend a lot of time watching basketball.

Spelling Workout: Check Plural Nouns

Fill in the blank with the correct plural form of the word in parentheses.

1. The pen-pal program gave me a list of _____ .
(match)

2. I picked up a couple of _____ to find the small town where my pen pal lives.
(atlas)

3. My pen pal and I exchange stories about our _____ .
(family)

4. He goes to a school that is just for _____ .
(boy)

5. My pen pal told us that he would like to visit _____ like New York and Washington, DC.
(city)

6. I would also like to visit other _____ and get to speak different _____ .
(country)
(language)

7. My pen pal always ends his letters with "Best _____ ."
(wish)

Editing and Proofreading in Action, continued

Mechanics Workout: Check Sentence Punctuation
Add correct end punctuation to each sentence.

1. I asked Carlos if I could come dressed as someone else instead

2. Did he really think I liked the idea of dressing up like a clown

3. It's going to be the best party ever

4. I decided to dress up like the Washington Monument

5. Will I need a lot of cardboard for my costume

Check Grammar, Spelling, and Mechanics
Proofread the passage. Check for correct sentences, the spelling of plural nouns, and sentence punctuation. Correct the mistakes.

Editing and Proofreading Marks	
∧	Insert something.
∧	Add a comma.
∧	Add a semicolon.
⊙	Add a period.
⊙	Add a colon.
ᵛ ᵛ	Add quotation marks.
ᵛ	Add apostrophe.
≡	Capitalize.
/	Make lower case.
℘	Delete.
¶	Make new paragraph.
◯	Check spelling.
⌒	Replace with this.
∿	Change order.
#	Insert space.
◡	Close up.

Looked at our watches and realized we had to hurry?
The party was in only a few hours and my costume was far
from finished. Carlos and his sister were all dressed up as
spys. Good choice. At first, those two had wanted to dress
as bunnys. Since used walkie-talkies, they also had to buy
batterys. I as the Washington Monument I needed at least
five cardboard boxs to assemble my costume, and now I
needed tape to fix the top.

"Do you have some extra tape!" I asked Carlos. When
Carlos looked at me, I could see the panic in his eyes. He so
much time taking care of his accessorys, had forgotten!

Editing and Proofreading in Action, continued

Edit and Proofread Your Personal Narrative

Now edit and proofread your work.

1. Use a checklist as you edit and proofread. Add things you are working on to the checklist.

2. Look to see which errors are marked most often. Jot down your top three trouble spots.

_____

_____

_____

Remember to Check

- ☐ correct sentences
- ☐ plural nouns
- ☐ sentence punctuation
- ☐ _____
- ☐ _____

3. Ask your teacher about ways to fix these mistakes, or check out the Grammar Handbook for information.

Focus on Spelling

Improve your spelling by following these steps.

1. Create a personal spelling list. Record words that you misspelled. Look up correct spellings in the dictionary and add these words to **My Spelling List**.

2. Pick twelve words. Make a colorful display of the words. Get a sheet of chart paper. Write each word three times in a different color.

3. Work with a partner to play **Spelling Tic-Tac-Toe**. Draw a tic-tac-toe board. Take turns asking each other to spell words. When a player spells a word correctly, that player gets to mark an X or an O on the game board.

4. Write the letters for each word on separate squares of paper. Attach the letters for each word to each other with a paper clip. Unscramble the letters to spell each of your words.

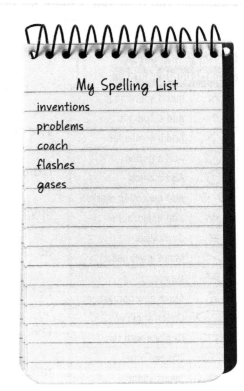

My Spelling List

inventions
problems
coach
flashes
gases

5. Invent your own memory strategy for difficult words. Think of a good way to remember *why* letters appear (or not) in a word. For example:

Word	Explanation
dessert	"It has two s's for **s**weet **s**tuff!"

Publish, Share, and Reflect

Publish and Share Your Personal Narrative

**Check the final formats you used to publish your personal narrative.
Then answer the following questions.**

Publishing

What was the final format of your project?	How did you share your project?
☐ Wrote it neatly by hand	☐ Shared it with a large group
☐ Typed it on a computer	☐ Shared it with a small group

1. Whether you published it by hand or on the computer, what did you do to dress up your final project?

_____

_____

_____

_____

_____

2. How did you share your work? What did you learn through sharing your work?

_____

_____

_____

_____

_____

_____

_____

_____

_____

_____

_____

_____

Reflect on Your Personal Narrative

Read your personal narrative. Then answer questions 1–6.

1. What do you like best about your work? _____

_____

_____

2. What did you do well? _____

_____

_____

3. What could you improve about your work? _____

_____

_____

_____

4. How did you choose to share your personal narrative? _____

_____

_____

5. What did you do to make your essay especially right for your audience? _____

_____

_____

6. Will you add your personal narrative to your Writing Portfolio? Explain
your decision.

❏ Yes, I will add this to my Writing Portfolio.

_____

_____

❏ No, I will not add this to my Writing Portfolio.

_____

_____

Analyze a Summary Paragraph

Read the article and each summary paragraph. Then answer the questions.

The African Lungfish
by Rupert Levin

The African lungfish challenges what we think about fish because this fish species can "hibernate" on land. The African lungfish has gills, like any ordinary fish. What makes the lungfish unique is that it also has a set of lungs, which allows it to live out of water.

The dry African climate in which the lungfish lives makes it necessary for it to have both gills and lungs. When water sources are available, the lungfish lives in the water and breathes through its gills. But when the water disappears during periods of drought, the lungfish uses its lungs to breathe. It digs a hole and buries itself. It curls into a ball lined with mucus and membranes, and breathes through its mouth. It can stay like that for an entire dry season.

Summary Paragraphs

A.   Robert Levin's article, "The African Lungfish," describes how the lungfish can live both on land and in water. In water, it breathes through gills. During the African dry season, it digs a hole. Then it curls into a ball and breathes through its mouth.

B.   The article tells about a fish that is unlike ordinary fish. It comes from Africa, which is a very dry place. It can breathe out of water and can live out of water for an entire dry season.

Feature Checklist

A good summary

☐ gives the title and the author of the work

☐ restates the writer's ideas in your own words

☐ includes all the main ideas and important details

☐ leaves out details that are not important.

1. **Which summary paragraph is a good summary? Explain your answer.**

   _____

   _____

   _____

   _____

   _____

2. **What can you say about the wording in the two summaries? Is it always original?**

   _____

   _____

   _____

   _____

   _____

3. **Do both summaries do a good job of leaving out details that are not important?**

   _____

   _____

   _____

   _____

   _____

Plan a Summary Paragraph

Use this page to plan your summary paragraph.

1. Read carefully the work you will be summarizing. If you're working with a copy you can mark up, underline or highlight important ideas as you read.

2. If you're working with a copy you can't mark up, use paper, your computer, or sticky notes to write down your ideas as you read.

3. Organize your notes using a web or diagram.

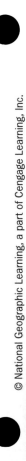

Draft a Summary Paragraph

Use your plan from page 32 to try a couple of different drafts of your summary paragraph.

Drafting Checklist

- ☐ Give the title and author of the work.
- ☐ Restate the writer's ideas in your own words.
- ☐ Include all the main ideas and important details.
- ☐ Leave out details that are not important.

Draft 1

_____

_____

_____

_____

_____

_____

_____

_____

Draft 2

_____

_____

_____

_____

_____

_____

_____

_____

Revise a Summary Paragraph

1. Use the checklist to evaluate this draft of a summary paragraph. What changes are needed?

_____

_____

_____

_____

_____

2. Revise this draft. Use revising marks to show your changes.

Revising	
MARK	**WHAT IT MEANS**
∧	Insert something.
↶	Move to here.
↶	Replace with this.
⟋	Take out.
¶	Make a new paragraph.

Armadillo Defenses

Susan Goodman's "On the Menu" describes different ways animals defend themselves against predators. One example she gives is armadillos. Armadillos are not good fighters because of their small teeth. The advantage the armadillo has is its armored shell. The shell is made of bony plates. The shell makes it difficult for predators to bite or injure an armadillo. When it's facing danger and cannot return to the safety of its burrow, the armadillo rolls up. Since many predators cannot get past the shell, the armadillo is safe. The hard shell completely covers its body.

3. Now use the checklist to help you revise the draft of your summary paragraph on page 33.

© National Geographic Learning, a part of Cengage Learning, Inc.

Edit and Proofread

Grammar Workout: Check Subject Pronouns

Fill in the blanks with the correct subject pronoun.

1. I read about pufferfish in Matt Galeano's article. _____ are a delicacy in countries like Japan.

2. A specially trained chef removes the parts containing tetrodotoxin. _____ has to be careful not to miss anything.

3. Tetrodotoxin is a deadly poison. _____ can be fatal even in small amounts.

4. Customers who eat the fish must really like it. _____ take a big risk to trust that the chefs removed all the poison!

5. When my sister and I go to Japan, _____ want to try the fish for ourselves!

Spelling Workout: Check Compound Words

Read each sentence. Circle the compound word that is written incorrectly. Then write the correct form in the blank.

1. Pufferfish are not thought to be fresh water fish, but not all species live in the ocean. _____

2. Large species of pufferfish use their beak to eat mussels and shell fish.

_____

3. In winter time, pufferfish have their highest levels of tetrodotoxin.

_____

4. There was another in-depth study of pufferfish in the news paper.

_____

5. Pufferfish are not exactly my favorite sea food. _____

6. I would only eat one if I were a cast away on a desert island.

_____

Mechanics Workout:
Check Capitalization of Proper Nouns

Use the editing marks below to correct the capitalization error(s) in each sentence.

1. monday was my birthday, and we went to a steakhouse where they serve

food from japan.

2. I asked michiko, our server, if the restaurant served pufferfish.

3. She said, "The united states is too far away from the part of the pacific ocean

where the fish are found."

4. I guess if I want to try eating pufferfish, I'll have to go to asia.

5. There's a cultural festival downtown next april—I wonder if they'll serve

pufferfish there.

Check Grammar, Spelling, and Mechanics

Proofread the passage. Check the compound words, the use of subject pronouns, and the capitalization of proper nouns. Correct the mistakes.

Editing and Proofreading Marks	
∧	Insert something.
∧	Add a comma.
∧	Add a semicolon.
⊙	Add a period.
⊙	Add a colon.
ᵛᵛ ᵛᵛ	Add quotation marks.
ᵛ	Add apostrophe.
≡	Capitalize.
/	Make lower case.
℘	Delete.
¶	Make new paragraph.
⬭	Check spelling.
⌒	Replace with this.
∿	Change order.
#	Insert space.
⌒	Close up.

The ocean view aquarium has just opened a new exhibit. They have just put three young pufferfish on display. The aquarium has many types of fish, but the pufferfish are the high-light of the exhibits. mr. simmons, our science teacher, read a news paper article about the pufferfish. She told us that the pufferfish will only be on display for 3 weeks. That's not much time! I'm going to visit there when-ever I have time.

Edit and Proofread, continued

Edit and Proofread Your Summary Paragraph

Now edit and proofread your work.

1. Use a checklist as you edit and proofread. Add things you are working on to the checklist.

2. Look to see which errors are marked most often. Jot down your top three trouble spots.

_____

_____

_____

3. Ask your teacher about ways to fix these mistakes, or check out the Grammar Handbook for information.

Focus on Spelling

Improve your spelling by following these steps.

1. Create a personal spelling list. Record words that you misspelled. Look up correct spelling in the dictionary and add these words to **My Spelling List**.

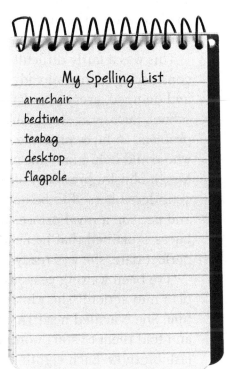

My Spelling List
armchair
bedtime
teabag
desktop
flagpole

2. Pick twelve words. Write six sentences, using two of the words in each sentence. Wacky sentences are just fine! Double-check the spelling. Then write six different sentences, using different pairs of spelling words.

3. Organize your words into different lists. List your words in alphabetical order. Next list them by the number of letters, from shortest word to longest. Spell the words aloud as you write them.

4. Make a personal word wall with your spelling words. List your words on chart paper. Read the words; then spell them. Next close your eyes and spell them again. Open your eyes. Did you spell the word correctly?

5. Invent a story to help you remember difficult words. For example:

Word: cemetery
Story: I got scared walking through the cemetery and yelled, "e-e-e!" as I ran away.
(The word *cemetery* has three e's.)

Analyze a Modern Fairy Tale

What makes this modern tale a good model?
Read the story and answer the questions.

A good modern tale includes

☐ interesting **characters**

☐ details for a modern **setting**

☐ recognizable **elements from an existing tale**

☐ a **conflict** a character has to solve

☐ a **plot** that makes the conflict worse until it comes to a turning point

☐ a satisfying resolution, or ending.

Finding His Queen

by Marisol Vásquez

Lucas Jablinsky ruled Southern Middle School. He was the boy every girl had a crush on, every guy wanted on his team, and every teacher wanted in his or her class. He received every award—academic and athletic—his school had to offer. The only award he had yet to claim was king of the eighth-grade dance. But he wasn't worried. He knew he would be chosen as the class king, and now he was on the lookout for the girl who would look almost as good as him that night.

This was a fairly difficult task, considering he had already dated, and dumped, every popular girl at school. Lucas was struggling with this problem, so he went to the one person who could help him—his mother. Mrs. Jablinsky, president of the PTA, considered herself to be queen bee, and her son a royal prince. When Lucas explained that he needed the perfect date, she was ready.

"I've been waiting years to put this plan into action!" she whispered to him. She e-mailed her PTA committee and told them to start working on a fashion show. Each eighth-grade girl would be given a dress to model in the show. Mrs. Jablinsky would personally sew each dress. What she didn't reveal was that in the waist of each dress she would sew a tiny knot. The model who felt uncomfortable in her dress would be worthy of being Lucas's date.

1. What makes Lucas interesting?

_____

_____

_____

_____

_____

_____

2. What are some details that make the setting modern?

_____

_____

_____

_____

_____

_____

3. What conflict does Lucas need to resolve?

_____

_____

_____

_____

_____

_____

Analyze a Modern Fairy Tale, continued

The day of the show arrived, and there was a buzz around the dressing room. Rumors flew about Mrs. Jablinsky searching for a date for Lucas. The girls eagerly donned their dresses. Each inspected her makeup. They also whispered about Isabella, the new girl in school, who apparently didn't care about getting a date with Lucas! She fidgeted in the corner, waiting for her turn on the auditorium stage. Underneath her cat-eye glasses were beautiful violet-colored eyes framed in long, curling lashes. The emerald green dress chosen for her set off her beautiful complexion. And, if she ever took her hair out of the bun it stayed knotted in, dark curls would cascade past her shoulders. She looked very uncomfortable backstage.

Each young lady took her turn on stage, smiling brightly in front of her peers and Mrs. Jablinsky. When Isabella came out from behind the curtain however, she struggled halfway across the stage and stopped with a sigh. "I'm sorry, but I can't pretend to be happy in this dress," she huffed. "There is something pinching my waist!" She rushed offstage.

Mrs. Jablinsky was ecstatic; she knew her plan had worked! She rushed to find Lucas. The two went in search of Isabella to tell her she was his lucky date! What a shock it was to them when Isabella smiled and said, politely, "No, thank you. If I am going to be queen, then I could never have a king who might upstage me!"

4. **What elements of an existing fairy tale do you recognize?**

_____

_____

_____

_____

_____

_____

_____

5. **How does the plot develop? How does the conflict get worse before it is resolved?**

_____

_____

_____

_____

_____

_____

_____

6. **Is there a satisfying ending? Why or why not?**

_____

_____

_____

_____

_____

_____

_____

Evaluate for Organization

Read each modern tale. Use the rubric on page 41 to score each sample for organization. Explain your scores.

Writing Sample 1

Red-Hooded Marcie

The wolf knew he could not fool Marcie if she could see him. He snuck into the maintenance room and turned out all of the lights. Luckily, he could see quite well in the dark. As soon as it went dark, he ran to the food court, where Marcie was supposed to meet Grandma. He waited.

After a little while, he saw her approaching. Her red hooded jacket was tied around her waist and she carried a shopping bag full of goodies from the candy store. "This will be easy," he thought as he sprayed on some of Grandma's perfume and stepped into Marcie's path.

Score	1	2	3	4

_____
_____
_____
_____
_____
_____
_____
_____
_____
_____
_____

Writing Sample 2

Marcie and the Wolf

The dark mall made Marcie feel afraid because she had never been to the mall so late at night before. Marcie felt relieved when her grandma's perfume wafted toward her nostrils. She reached out, took her grandma's hand, and started chatting about what she bought. Grandma grunted in response and sneered back at Marcie. Marcie didn't understand her grandma's reaction, but she continued to walk quickly to the door. Marcie ran away and hid beneath one of the tables in the food court. She could hear the wolf approaching quietly. Marcie ate a piece of candy from her bag and got an idea. She threw all her candy at the wolf. The wolf yelped and scurried away. Marcie went to find her grandma, and she was saved.

Score	1	2	3	4

_____
_____
_____
_____
_____
_____
_____
_____
_____
_____
_____

Evaluate for Organization, continued

Writing Rubric		
Organization		
	Does the writing have a clear structure, and is it appropriate for the writer's audience, purpose, and type of writing?	**How smoothly do the ideas flow together?**
4 Wow!	The writing has a structure that is <u>clear</u> and appropriate for the writer's audience, purpose, and type of writing.	The ideas progress in a smooth and orderly way. • The introduction is strong. • The **ideas** flow well from **paragraph** to **paragraph**. • The ideas in each paragraph flow well from one **sentence** to the next. • Effective **transitions** connect ideas. • The conclusion is strong.
3 Ahh.	The writing has a structure that is <u>generally</u> clear and appropriate for the writer's audience, purpose, and type of writing.	<u>Most</u> of the ideas progress in a smooth and orderly way. • The introduction is adequate. • Most of the **ideas** flow well from **paragraph** to **paragraph**. • Most ideas in each paragraph flow from one **sentence** to the next. • Effective **transitions** connect most of the ideas. • The conclusion is adequate.
2 Hmm.	The structure of the writing is <u>not</u> clear or <u>not</u> appropriate for the writer's audience, purpose, and type of writing.	<u>Some</u> of the ideas progress in a smooth and orderly way. • The introduction is weak. • Some of the **ideas** flow well from **paragraph** to **paragraph**. • Some ideas in each paragraph flow from one **sentence** to the next. • **Transitions** connect some ideas. • The conclusion is weak.
1 Huh?	The writing is not clear or organized.	<u>Few or none</u> of the ideas progress in a smooth and orderly way.

41

Raise the Score

1. Use the rubric on page 41 to evaluate and score this modern tale.

Score	1	2	3	4

Sophie and the Frog

Sophie and her sister Estella were depressed because the big school dance was only a week away.

Estella walked to the mall and she heard a voice. "Excuse me," the voice said. "Will you go to the dance with me?"

A frog was speaking, and it was all Estella could do to control her laughter. "Are you crazy?" she cried. "You're a frog, and you're disgusting."

Sophie heard a voice coming from the grass. She was at soccer practice, but she was taking a water break. It was the same frog who'd talked to Estella. "Hi there," said the frog. "Will you go to the dance with me?"

Sophie considered the frog's question, and she agreed to go to the dance with the frog, even though going out with a frog was a little weird.

"Great," said the frog; "I'll pick you up at seven."

"I can't believe you're going out with a frog," said Estella. "That's so gross."

The doorbell rang. The frog, wearing a tux, was holding a bouquet of flowers for Sophie.

Estella laughed at Sophie, but Sophie didn't pay any attention. Instead, she decided to kiss the frog on the cheek. The frog turned into a handsome young man!

"This is so unfair!" Estella cried.

2. Explain what the writer should do to raise the score:

_____

_____

_____

_____

_____

_____

_____

_____

_____

Raise the Score, continued

3. **Now revise the passage on page 42 to improve organization.**
   Write your revised passage here.

_____

_____

_____

_____

_____

_____

_____

_____

_____

_____

_____

_____

_____

_____

_____

_____

_____

_____

_____

_____

_____

_____

_____

_____

_____

_____

_____

_____

_____

Use Transitions

Use the sentences below, along with transition words and other sentences of your own, to tell the story of Tiffany's Magic Trumpet.

- Tiffany bought a trumpet that could play on its own.

- She did not practice playing the trumpet.

- Tiffany's music teacher asked Tiffany to play the last part of a song for a test.

- Tiffany's trumpet would only play the song from the beginning.

- Tiffany's music teacher gave Tiffany a failing grade.

- Tiffany sold her trumpet on the Internet and bought a regular trumpet.

- Tiffany practiced until she could play the song well.

- Tiffany's music teacher let her do a retest.

Some Transition Words	
Cause	**Time**
because	one day
since	earlier
as a result	before
Order	**Emphasis**
first	in fact
then	more important
finally	amazingly
Examples	**Contrast**
for instance	although
for example	but
as you can see	however
Comparison	**Summary**
also	all in all
likewise	finally
similarly	in the end

_____

_____

_____

_____

_____

_____

_____

_____

_____

_____

_____

_____

_____

_____

_____

_____

Use Transitions, continued

Read each story starter. Continue the story using transition words to connect the ideas.

The Magic Basketball

1.   Ali loved to play basketball, but he was a horrible player. He practiced all the time, but he never seemed to improve. One day, he saw a strange-looking basketball lying in the bushes. "I wish I were the best basketball player in school," he said.

Amazingly, _____

_____

_____

_____

_____

_____

_____

_____

_____

_____

_____

Henry and Greta

2.   Henry and Greta were on a camping trip with their family. They decided to climb Andersen Peak, but they were worried they wouldn't be able to find their way back to their campsite.

As a result, _____

_____

_____

_____

_____

_____

_____

_____

_____

_____

Connect Your Paragraphs

Read the passage. Tie the paragraphs together by adding transitions.

Some Transition Words			
Cause	**Time**	**Order**	**Emphasis**
because	one day	first	in fact
since	earlier	then	more important
as a result	before	finally	amazingly
Examples	**Contrast**	**Comparison**	**Summary**
for instance	although	also	all in all
for example	but	likewise	finally
as you can see	however	similarly	in the end

The Three Brothers

Three brothers decided to build a fort in their backyard, but they could not come to an agreement about which materials to use to construct their fort. Max wanted to use bricks, Jacob wanted to use wood, and Cody wanted to use concrete blocks.

A huge fight broke out among the brothers. Each brother thought his material was the best. After a while, their father stepped in to settle the matter. He told them that they would just have to build separate forts.

Each brother set out to construct his own fort. Jacob used some of his dad's firewood that was stacked by the house. Max found some bricks to use for his fort. Cody found some concrete blocks.

They finished building their forts and decided to test them out by climbing inside. Each brother congratulated himself on a job well done.

The brothers were in for a surprise. As he sat in his fort, Jacob heard a knock on its wooden door. "Who's there?" he called.

Plan a Modern Fairy Tale

Use pages 47–49 to plan your modern fairy tale.

1. Think about your characters and setting. Who is your story about?
Where and when does it take place?

Setting: _____

Character	What he or she is like

2. Now, start to plan your plot. What's the problem that your characters
will face? Write a few sentences about the problem.

_____

_____

_____

_____

3. Plan your plot. What will happen in the beginning, middle, and ending?
Jot down your ideas on the plot diagram.

Plot Diagram

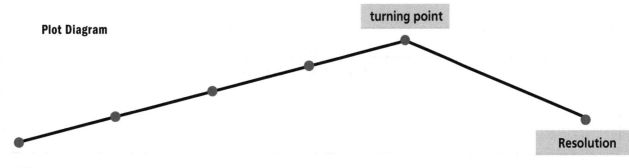

turning point

Resolution

4. Now it's time to flesh out your plot with details. Use the organizer to develop details for each part of your story.

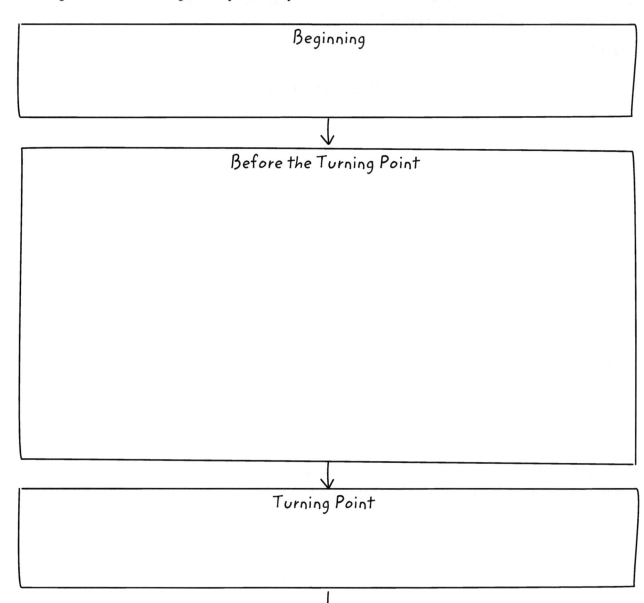

Beginning

Before the Turning Point

Turning Point

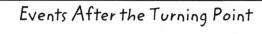

Events After the Turning Point

Ending (Resolution)

Plan a Modern Fairy Tale, continued

5. Fill out the Five-Senses Diagram to plan how you'll use sensory details to show what happens and what the characters are like.

My character saw . . .	
My character heard . . .	
My character smelled . . .	
My character tasted . . .	
My character felt . . .	

Use the chart to plan details and dialogue with which you'll reveal a lot about your characters without telling your reader.

Detail	What it means:

Draft a Modern Fairy Tale

Use your plan from pages 47–49 to write the first draft of your modern fairy tale.

Use your plan from pages 47–49 to write the first draft of your modern fairy tale.

Drafting Checklist

- ☐ Create a main character and other interesting characters.
- ☐ Describe the setting.
- ☐ Include recognizable elements from an existing tale.
- ☐ Give the main character a conflict to solve.
- ☐ Develop an exciting plot and include a turning point.
- ☐ Show, don't tell your characters' motives and emotions.
- ☐ Use transitions to make your ideas flow.
- ☐ End with a satisfying resolution.

© National Geographic Learning, a part of Cengage Learning, Inc.

Draft a Modern Fairy Tale, continued

Revise a Modern Fairy Tale

1. Use the checklist to evaluate this draft of a modern fairy tale. What changes are needed?

_____

_____

_____

_____

_____

Revising Checklist

☐ Do you need to add sensory details to help your reader picture the events?

☐ Do the events flow in logical order?

☐ Would adding transition words improve the flow of your story?

☐ Should you rearrange any sentence or paragraphs?

2. Revise this draft. Use revising marks to show your changes.

Revising

MARK	WHAT IT MEANS
∧	Insert something.
↶	Move to here.
∧̅	Replace with this.
↗	Take out.
¶	Make a new paragraph.

Erica's First Dance

Erica was excited because she was attending her first school dance. She spent her whole day getting ready. She bought a new dress, and she curled her hair and pinned it on top of her head. Lisa wasn't home. Erica couldn't wait and sneaked into Lisa's bedroom. The only thing she was missing was earrings, and Erica was sure her sister Lisa had the perfect pair. The first pair was the wrong color. The second pair was too small. The third pair was perfect. She saw her sister watching her.

3. Now use the checklist to help you revise the draft of your modern tale on pages 50–52.

Edit and Proofread

Grammar Workout: Check Subject-Verb Agreement

Complete each sentence with the correct form of *have* or *be*.

1. Anansi _____ to do something to help the townspeople.
(have)

2. The townspeople _____ sick of living in silence and need
Anansi's help.   (be)

3. The townspeople wondered, "_____ Anansi clever enough to
outsmart Mr. Nyame?"   (be)

4. The townspeople cried, "We _____ to believe in Anansi. We can't do
anything else."   (have)

5. "I _____ sure that Anansi won't be able to fool me!" exclaimed Mr. Nyame.
(be)

6. "Mr. Nyame _____ a point," said Anansi, his eye twinkling with
mischief.   (have)

Spelling Workout: Check Two-Syllable Words

**Use your knowledge of the VCCV and VCV pattern to correctly spell each
misspelled common word.**

1. helo   _____

2. ofice   _____

3. pollite   _____

4. babby   _____

5. matress   _____

6. hottel   _____

7. dady   _____

8. patern   _____

9. ovver   _____

10. botom   _____

11. studdent   _____

12. ribon   _____

13. chalenge   _____

14. vilage   _____

15. comon   _____

16. tigger   _____

Edit and Proofread, continued

Mechanics Workout: Check Capitalization and Punctuation

Use proofreading marks to correct the capitalization and punctuation of each sentence.

1. Anansi said to himself "if I want my words back, I'll have to get them myself".

2. To Mr. Nyame he said "you do not have the right to our words!

3. Mr. Nyame replied you want your words back? It will cost you dearly"!

Check Grammar, Spelling, and Mechanics

Proofread the passage. Check the spelling, subject-verb agreement, and capitalization and punctuation of dialogue. Correct the mistakes.

Editing and Proofreading Marks	
∧	Insert something.
∧	Add a comma.
∧	Add a semicolon.
⊙	Add a period.
⊙	Add a colon.
✌ ✌	Add quotation marks.
✓	Add apostrophe.
≡	Capitalize.
/	Make lower case.
℘	Delete.
¶	Make new paragraph.
◯	Check spelling.
⌒	Replace with this.
∽	Change order.
#	Insert space.
◡	Close up.

Mr. Nyame had never been outsmarted before. I has to find a way to get those words back" he said to himself. "The people's talking and laughing is driving me crazzy"!

Mr. Nyame grabbed his voice-catcher from his shelf and ventured out into the town. Each time he heard someone speak, he opened the voice-catcher and captured the sound. After a few hours, Mr. Nyame listened carefully. Silence! "That's beter" he thought. Then he saw Anansi sitting on a stool in the courtyard. Anansi's voice had not been captured.

"Mr. Nyame," Anansi shouted you may have won the batle, but I is going to win the war. I will find a way to get the people's voices back!"

Edit and Proofread Your Modern Fairy Tale

Now edit and proofread your work.

1. Use a checklist as you edit and proofread. Add things you are working on to the checklist.

2. Look to see which errors are marked most often. Jot down your top three trouble spots.

_____

_____

_____

3. Ask your teacher about ways to fix these mistakes, or check out the Grammar Handbook for information.

Focus on Spelling

Improve your spelling by following these steps.

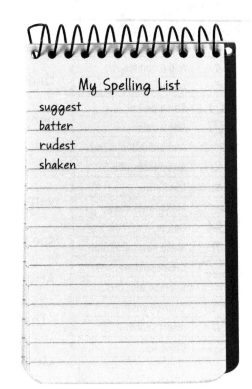

My Spelling List
suggest
batter
rudest
shaken

1. Create a personal spelling list. Record words that you misspelled. Look up correct spelling in the dictionary and add these words to **My Spelling List**.

2. Pick twelve words. Write each word four times. First write it in lowercase letters. Next write it in capital letters. Then write the vowels in lowercase and the consonants in capitals. Last, write the word using fancy letters. For example, your letters can be curly, or tall and skinny.

3. Work with a partner to play **I'm Thinking of a Spelling Word**. Take turns giving each other clues. Some clues might be _I'm thinking of a word that rhymes with . . ., I'm thinking of a word that begins with . . .,_ or _I'm thinking of a word that means . . ._ With each clue, the answer should include the word and its spelling.

4. Work with a partner to play a scrambled-letter game. Take each other's spelling words and write them in scrambled form. See which one of you can unscramble all the words first.

5. Use an audio recorder and record your words and their spelling. Then listen to your recording, checking to see that you spelled each word correctly.

Publish, Share, and Reflect

Publish and Share Your Modern Tale

**Check the final formats you used to publish your modern tale.
Then answer the following questions.**

Publishing
What was the final format of your project?	**How did you share your project?**
☐ Wrote it neatly by hand	☐ Shared it with a large group
☐ Typed it on a computer	☐ Shared it with a small group

1. Whether you published it by hand or on the computer, what did you do to dress up your final project?

_____

_____

_____

_____

_____

2. How did you share your work? What did you learn through sharing your work?

_____

_____

_____

_____

_____

_____

_____

_____

_____

_____

_____

Reflect on Your Modern Tale

Read your modern tale. Then answer questions 1–6.

1. What do you like best about your work? _____

_____

_____

2. What did you do well? _____

_____

_____

3. What could you improve about your work? _____

_____

_____

_____

4. What did you learn about developing a plot? _____

_____

_____

5. What was the hardest part of creating characters? _____

_____

_____

6. Will you add your modern tale to your Writing Portfolio?
   Explain your decision.

   ☐ Yes, I will add this to my Writing Portfolio.

   _____

   _____

   ☐ No, I will not add this to my Writing Portfolio.

   _____

   _____

Analyze a Problem-and-Solution Paragraph

What makes this problem-and-solution paragraph a good model? Read the paragraph and answer the questions.

Make It Colorful!

by Marcus Smith

Why does our school have to look so drab and boring? I'm not very awake when I get to school, and the dull green walls certainly don't inspire me to walk inside. When we go outside at lunch, the scenery is nonexistent. All we see are patches of brown grass and gray concrete. If educators and parents want to get us excited about going to school, we should at least have interesting surroundings. It wouldn't be too difficult to send out flyers to everyone in the school and the community asking for plants and flowers. Many landscapers probably have leftover plants they could donate. They may even volunteer to plant them. And, we can look for recycled paints in the town dump. New and colorful paints will jazz up the exterior walls. With just those few changes, I guarantee we'll all arrive at school with a lot more enthusiasm!

Feature Checklist

A good problem-and-solution paragraph

☐ presents a problem

☐ offers and supports an effective solution.

1. **What problem does the writer describe?**

_____

_____

_____

_____

_____

_____

2. **What reasons does the writer give for why the school's looks are important?**

_____

_____

_____

_____

_____

_____

_____

3. **What solutions to the problem does the writer suggest?**

_____

_____

_____

_____

_____

_____

_____

Plan a Problem-and-Solution Paragraph

Use pages 60–61 to plan your problem-and-solution paragraph.

1. Write down some problems that you have solved or have some idea about how to solve. Then circle the one you care the most about.

Ideas

2. Narrow your topic to make it specific.

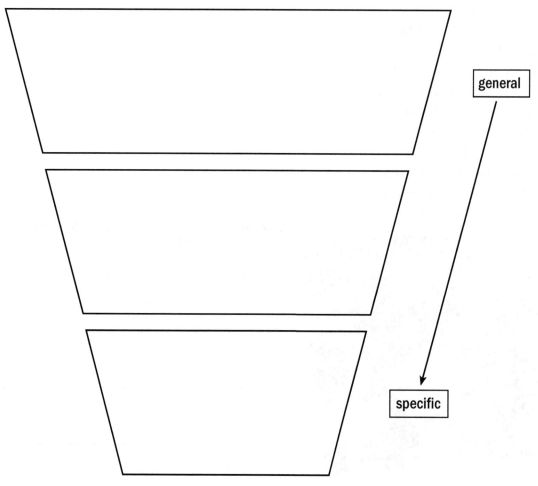

general

specific

Plan a Problem-and-Solution Paragraph, continued

3. Gather the details about your problem and solution. Use the chart.

Problem and Solution	Reasons and Evidence

4. Use the "road map" to organize your ideas and develop the plan for your paragraph.

Step 1: Identify the problem

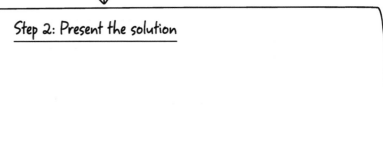

Step 2: Present the solution

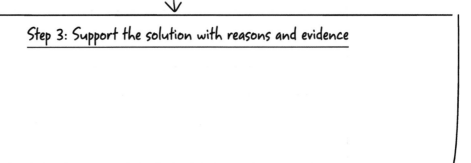

Step 3: Support the solution with reasons and evidence

Problem-and-Solution Map

Draft a Problem-and-Solution Paragraph

Use your plan from pages 60–61 to write the first draft of your problem-and-solution paragraph.

Drafting Checklist

- ☐ Identify the problem clearly in your topic sentence.
- ☐ Present the solution.
- ☐ Support the solution with reasons and evidence.

Revise a Problem-and-Solution Paragraph

1. Use the checklist to evaluate this draft of a problem-and-solution paragraph. What changes are needed?

_____

_____

_____

_____

_____

Revising Checklist

☐ Is your problem clearly stated?

☐ Does your solution seem reasonable?

☐ Does the paragraph start with the problem, then present the solution?

☐ Is there any unnecessary information that should be removed?

2. Revise the draft. Use revising marks to show your changes.

Revising

MARK	WHAT IT MEANS
∧	Insert something.
↶	Move to here.
∧	Replace with this.
﹍	Take out.
¶	Make a new paragraph.

Breakfast in the Cafeteria

Many students arrive at our school very early in the morning. Some of them come early because their buses arrive before eight o'clock. These students are not able to eat breakfast. This is a problem because students should have the option to eat breakfast at school. Nutritionists say that breakfast is the most important meal of the day. The solution to this problem is simple. We can ask the cafeteria manager to make breakfast available to students who want it. We should survey all students who arrive at school early.

3. Now use the checklist to help you revise the draft of your problem-and-solution paragraph on page 62. Use a clean sheet of paper.

Edit and Proofread

Grammar Workout: Check Verbs in the Past Tense

Complete each sentence. Write the past tense of the verb in parentheses.

1. Every day we _____ about the unfairness of our school's lunch policy. **(talk)**

2. We _____ our school to allow eighth graders to eat lunch in the courtyard. **(petition)**

3. Students _____ the unfair treatment of eighth graders. **(protest)**

4. We even _____ staging a sit-in. **(consider)**

5. Thankfully, the principal _____ to all our complaints. **(listen)**

Spelling Workout: Check Verbs with –ed and –ing

Circle the spelling mistake in each sentence. Then write the word correctly.

1. We were proposeing a new idea for lunchtime. _____

2. The students planed their petition together. _____

3. Last month, we examind the life of Thurgood Marshall; his story inspired us to stand up for our rights. _____

4. Our teacher was encourageing us to make our voices heard. _____

5. Even some parents were leanning toward signing. _____

Edit and Proofread, continued

Mechanics Workout: Check Capitalization of Proper Nouns

Use proofreading marks to correct the capitalization errors in the sentences below.

1. Because our petition was successful, other students at Walt Whitman middle school decided to start their own protests.

2. Now, the smart snacks club is requesting that they be allowed to eat snacks during Science Class.

3. Our principal, Ms. Linda sue Huong, believes that food should not be in the classroom.

4. She spoke with Representatives of the Walt Whitman student association.

5. She explained that eating food during a Teacher's instruction is distracting.

Check Grammar, Spelling, and Mechanics

Proofread the passage. Check the past-tense verbs, verbs with –ed and –ing, and capitalization of proper nouns. Correct the mistakes.

Editing and Proofreading Marks

Mark	Meaning
∧	Insert something.
∧	Add a comma.
∧	Add a semicolon.
⊙	Add a period.
⊙	Add a colon.
ᵛᵛ ᵛᵛ	Add quotation marks.
ᵛ	Add apostrophe.
≡	Capitalize.
/	Make lower case.
℘	Delete.
¶	Make new paragraph.
◯	Check spelling.
⌒	Replace with this.
∾	Change order.
#	Insert space.
⌒	Close up.

Last month, students from Rosa parks Middle School in jackson county joind in a project. The students were geting tired of the unhealthy food served in the cafeteria. So, they decide to write a petition to plant a Community garden. Students would use the produce from the garden in the Cafeteria. Yesterday, Oliver morrison, President of the Student Association, announces that he's meetting with mayor Robbins to discuss plans for the garden in the town's empty lot.

Edit and Proofread Your Problem-and-Solution Paragraph

Now edit and proofread your work.

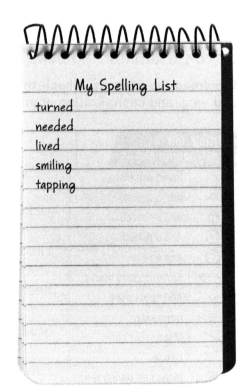

Remember to Check

☐ verbs in the past tense
☐ verbs with −ed and −ing
☐ capitalization of proper nouns
☐ _____
☐ _____

1. Use a checklist as you edit and proofread. Add things you are working on to the checklist.

2. Look to see which errors are marked most often. Jot down your top three trouble spots.

_____

_____

_____

3. Ask your teacher about ways to fix these mistakes, or check out the Grammar Handbook for information.

Focus on Spelling

Improve your spelling by following these steps.

1. Create a personal spelling list. Record words that you misspelled. Look up correct spelling in the dictionary and add these words to **My Spelling List**.

My Spelling List
turned
needed
lived
smiling
tapping

2. Pick twelve words. Make a colorful display of the words. Get a sheet of chart paper. Write each word three times in a different color.

3. Work with a partner to play **Spelling Tic-Tac-Toe**. Draw a tic-tac-toe board. Take turns asking each other to spell words. When a player spells a word correctly, that player gets to mark an X or an O on the game board.

4. Write the letters for each word on separate squares of paper. Attach the letters for each word to each other with a paper clip. Unscramble the letters to spell each of your words.

5. Invent your own memory strategy for difficult words. Think of a good way to remember *why* letters appear (or not) in a word. For example

Word	Explanation
dessert	"It has two s's for <u>s</u>weet <u>s</u>tuff!"

Analyze a Problem-and-Solution Essay

What makes this problem-and-solution essay a good model? Read the problem-and-solution essay and answer the questions.

Students Helping Students
by Ralph J. Rubin

Low test scores at Albert Einstein Middle School are a major problem. It would benefit students greatly if a Tutor Center was organized at our school.

According to the school administration, nearly 25 percent of the student body received failing grades on tests last month in one or more of their classes. Albert Einstein Middle School has classes that contain students with mixed abilities. In this type of environment, there will always be students who grasp the material and students who do not. Our class sizes are so large that teachers do not have the time to give struggling students one-on-one attention. As a result, some students do not get a clear understanding of what's being taught. Then they don't perform well on the tests. Our school does not have any programs that provide extra help and support for those who need it. Struggling students are often left on their own to figure things out. This is no way to learn anything. Without extra help students will continue to do poorly on exams. Some will even be in danger of failing their classes.

Feature Checklist

A good problem-and-solution essay

- ☐ presents a problem and a solution
- ☐ discusses the reasons for needing to solve the problem
- ☐ gives evidence for why the solution works and how to make it happen
- ☐ summarizes important points.

1. What makes the first paragraph a good introduction?

_____

_____

_____

_____

2. What claim does the writer make? How does he suggest the problem can be solved?

_____

_____

_____

_____

_____

_____

3. Why does the writer feel that this problem should be solved?

_____

_____

_____

_____

A Tutor Center would give struggling students a chance to get extra help with difficult subjects. Statistics have shown that tutoring can raise student scores by up to two letter grades. The Tutor Center could open its doors immediately after school. Hiring professional tutors can be expensive, but using volunteers can reduce many of the costs. Teacher or parent volunteers could supervise the program. Students who are doing well on tests and in the classroom could serve as the tutors. Struggling students would come to the center and be paired with a tutor. The tutor would provide the student with one-on-one attention and support. Struggling students could get help with their homework assignments or study for upcoming tests. Students could also ask their tutors for study and memory tips that would help them on tests. Tutors could ask classroom teachers to provide practice tests and exams so that students can be better prepared. These measures would help struggling students raise their test scores. It would also help them feel more confident and relaxed when taking tests.

A Tutor Center would benefit all students at Albert Einstein Middle School. Struggling students will have a place to go to receive extra help with their schoolwork. This extra help will surely raise the student body's test scores.

4. **What is the purpose of the third paragraph?**

_____

_____

_____

_____

_____

5. **How does the writer anticipate objections to the cost of a Tutor Center?**

_____

_____

_____

_____

6. **Why does the writer believe his solution will work?**

_____

_____

_____

_____

_____

_____

7. **What is good about the conclusion?**

_____

_____

_____

_____

_____

Evaluate for Focus and Unity

Read each problem-and-solution essay. Use the rubric on page 70 to score each essay for **focus and unity**. Explain your scores.

Writing Sample 1

The Budget Problem

Budget cuts at our school are forcing the principal to cancel after-school activities. Because of rising energy costs, the school must sacrifice after-school activities to add more money to the budget. To help save on energy costs and save our activities, our school should go "green."

Conserving energy is easy to do, and it will help us save money. As a school, we waste a lot of energy by keeping classroom lights on when they're not in use. Turning the lights off can help save on the costs of electricity. Our principal could also invest part of our limited budget to make our building more energy-efficient. In this case, spending money will help us save money in the long run. We can save more than 30% on our bills by going "green." This will give us the money we need to save our programs.

Going green will allow us to restore our extra activities.

Score	1	2	3	4

_____
_____
_____
_____
_____
_____
_____
_____
_____

Writing Sample 2

Extra Activities

Our school is canceling extra activities. Many students are sad about this.

Many students stay after school for photography classes, and to play in the jazz band. I play in the jazz band. Have you heard us? We're really good! The Student Association thinks the school could raise money by holding fundraisers. We can also have volunteers come in after hours and teach for free.

I think these are smart ideas, and I really hope the principal takes them into consideration.

Score	1	2	3	4

_____
_____
_____
_____
_____
_____
_____
_____

Writing Rubric

Focus and Unity

	How clearly does the writing present a central idea or claim?	How well does everything go together?
4 Wow!	The writing expresses a <u>clear</u> central idea or claim about the topic.	<u>Everything</u> in the writing goes together. • The main idea of each paragraph goes with the central idea or claim of the paper. • The main idea and details within each paragraph are related. • The conclusion is about the central idea or claim.
3 Ahh.	The writing expresses a <u>generally</u> clear central idea or claim about the topic.	<u>Most</u> parts of the writing go together. • The main idea of most paragraphs goes with the central idea or claim of the paper. • In most paragraphs, the main idea and details are related. • Most of the conclusion is about the central idea or claim.
2 Hmm.	The writing includes a topic, but the central idea or claim is <u>not</u> clear.	<u>Some</u> parts of the writing go together. • The main idea of some paragraphs goes with the central idea or claim of the paper. • In some paragraphs, the main idea and details are related. • Some of the conclusion is about the central idea or claim.
1 Huh?	The writing includes many topics and <u>does not</u> express one central idea or claim.	The parts of the writing <u>do not</u> go together. • Few paragraphs have a main idea, or the main idea does not go with the central idea or claim of the paper. • Few paragraphs contain a main idea and related details. • None of the conclusion is about the central idea or claim..

Raise the Score

1. Use the rubric on page 70 to evaluate and score this problem-and-solution essay.

Score	1	2	3	4

How to Save the Drama Class

This year's drama class will be canceled. There were budget cuts, and the principal had to cancel the class. Drama students are very upset because they were working on a production of William Shakespeare's *A Midsummer Night's Dream.*

Initially, the budget for the production was high. This allowed for many props and fancy costumes. Students wanted fake trees and a variety of costumes for the kings, queens, and fairies. This is not possible anymore.

The drama class can go on with a new teacher. Actors from the Old Burbage Company are willing to help. They've staged many Shakespearean plays recently, and they always got great reviews. They could lead workshops in our school every week.

A Midsummer Night's Dream is a complex play with many characters. It is also one of William Shakespeare's most famous plays. Students can go to the library and study previous representations of the play. They could find inexpensive ideas for how to stage the play. Another good idea would be to set up comedy skits to raise money. Even $2 tickets will be helpful, and then people might be willing to give even more.

Other extra activities can be canceled due to the budget cut. I believe that students can find creative ways to solve this problem.

2. Explain what the writer should do to raise the score:

_____

_____

_____

_____

3. **Now revise the problem-and-solution essay on page 71 to improve its focus and unity. Write your revised problem-and-solution essay here.**

State a Claim

1. Think about the topic. Then evaluate each claim. Explain your answer.

Topic: I'm writing about the problem of uninformed students.

Claim	Too Broad	Too Narrow	Just Right	Why?
Students should have a way of finding out what's going on at school.				_____ _____ _____ _____
To help students know what's going on at school, we should have a student newspaper.				_____ _____ _____ _____
To help students know the weekly specials in the cafeteria, we should have a student newspaper.				_____ _____ _____ _____ _____

2. **Study the information for each essay. Then write a claim for the essay.**

Topic: *School mess*

Problem: *The school hallways and lunch areas are covered with trash because students litter.*

Solution: *Students should be fined for littering.*

Claim:

_____

_____

_____

_____

Topic: *School lockers*

Problem: *School lockers are too small for band or orchestra instruments. Student musicians must carry their instruments with them to class.*

Solution: *The school should install separate lockers in the music room.*

Claim:

_____

_____

_____

_____

Topic: *Crosswalk*

Problem: *There is not a crosswalk at Main Street and Ivy Avenue. Many students cross at this intersection and run the risk of being hit by a car.*

Solution: *A crosswalk should be installed at the intersection. A crossing guard should also be on duty.*

Claim:

_____

_____

_____

_____

Stay Focused on the Claim

1. Study the diagram. Use it to figure out how you would fix the focus of the problem-and-solution essay.

Essay Diagram

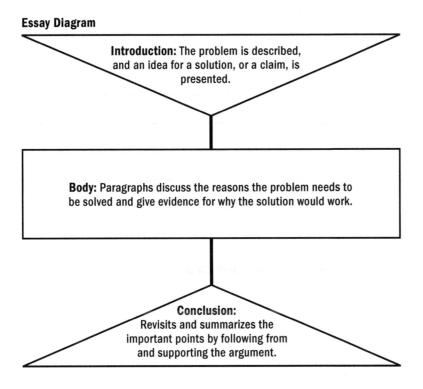

Introduction: The problem is described, and an idea for a solution, or a claim, is presented.

Body: Paragraphs discuss the reasons the problem needs to be solved and give evidence for why the solution would work.

Conclusion: Revisits and summarizes the important points by following from and supporting the argument.

Problem-and-Solution Essay

A New Town, A New School

Did you make good friends in school? Being the new kid at school is never easy, especially when you *are* the new kid every few years. This is the case for children in military families.

Children in military families have a tough time. Every time their parents are transferred to another city, they have to follow. They can move to cities that are close to each other. But often, they have to move far away. This means these children have to get used to a new city, a new house, new teachers, and new friends. Sometimes, the change can be overwhelming.

MacFarland Middle School is a respected institution in our area. In order to help these students, MacFarland Middle School has devised a plan. Each new student receives a welcome packet with all kinds of information on the school. This year, student representative Francis Michaels is in charge of assembling the welcome packet. The school offers many interesting extra activities. Then, the student is paired with a volunteer student. The pairing is done based on the interests of the child. This way, the school hopes the newcomer will make new friends more easily.

Changing schools can be daunting, but many schools are trying to help.

2. How would you fix the introduction for "A New Town, A New School"? Explain.

_____

_____

_____

_____

_____

_____

_____

_____

_____

3. How would you make each paragraph in the essay stay focused on a claim? Describe two things you can do.

_____

_____

_____

_____

_____

_____

_____

_____

_____

_____

4. Is the conclusion complete? Is it about a claim? Write a new conclusion.

_____

_____

_____

_____

_____

_____

_____

_____

_____

Plan a Problem-and-Solution Essay

Use pages 77–78 to plan your problem-and-solution essay.

1. Record some problems in your school or community. Then choose one to write about.

Problem	Solution

2. Write a claim for your introduction at the top of the **essay diagram**.

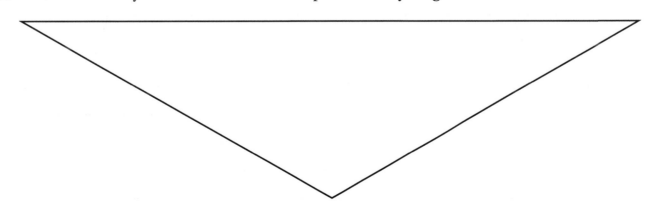

© National Geographic Learning, a part of Cengage Learning, Inc.

3. Map out the body of your essay in the diagram.

Paragraph 2

Topic: _____

_____

_____

Reason/Evidence: _____   Reason/Evidence: _____   Reason/Evidence: _____

_____   _____   _____

_____   _____   _____

_____   _____   _____

_____   _____   _____

_____   _____   _____

Paragraph 3

Topic: _____

_____

_____

Reason/Evidence: _____   Reason/Evidence: _____   Reason/Evidence: _____

_____   _____   _____

_____   _____   _____

_____   _____   _____

_____   _____   _____

_____   _____   _____

Draft a Problem-and-Solution Essay

Use your plan from pages 77–78 to write the first draft of your problem-and-solution essay.

Drafting Checklist

- ☐ Present a problem and a solution in the introduction.
- ☐ Express a clear claim.
- ☐ Include a topic and reasons and evidence in each paragraph of the body that support the claim.
- ☐ Use credible sources to argue why your solution works.
- ☐ Summarize the important points in the conclusion.

_____
_____
_____
_____
_____
_____
_____
_____
_____
_____
_____
_____
_____
_____
_____
_____
_____
_____
_____
_____
_____
_____
_____
_____
_____
_____
_____
_____
_____
_____

Revise a Problem-and-Solution Essay

1. Use the checklist to evaluate this draft of a problem-and-solution essay. What changes are needed?

_____

_____

_____

_____

_____

Revising Checklist
☐ Does the essay identify a problem and present a solution?
☐ Does the essay have a conclusion?
☐ Do any details need to be rearranged to clarify ideas?
☐ Are all the details necessary?

2. Revise the draft. Use revising marks to show your changes.

Revising	
MARK	**WHAT IT MEANS**
∧	Insert something.
↶	Move to here.
∧	Replace with this.
_ə	Take out.
¶	Make a new paragraph.

Making a Difference

I was really excited about my new school, until I got there. The grounds were so disgusting that I asked my teacher if the school had a cleanup club. He said it didn't, but suggested I create one. There was trash on the ground all around school. This was not only bad for the environment, but also bad for the morale of the school. During the first meeting, we cleaned up the grounds around school. Most of the trash was soda cans. Students wanted to know how they could help. Now we clean up areas in the community and take more pride in our school.

3. Now use the checklist to help you revise the draft of your problem-and-solution essay on pages 79–80. Use a clean sheet of paper.

Edit and Proofread

Grammar Workout: Check Irregular Past Tense Verbs

Rewrite each sentence. Use the past tense form of the verbs.

1. A representative of the Welcome! Group speaks to the teachers and gets their support.

_____

_____

2. Thanks to the Welcome! Group, life for a foreign exchange student becomes much easier.

_____

_____

3. The news about the upcoming welcome party spreads very quickly.

_____

_____

4. The exchange students tell me how much they appreciate the party.

_____

_____

Spelling Workout: Check Prefixes and Suffixes

Add the prefix _un-_ to these words.

1. necessary _____   **2.** organized _____   **3.** reasonable _____

Add the suffix _-able_ to these words.

4. vary _____   **5.** advise _____   **6.** remove _____

Add the suffix _-ness_ to these words.

7. crazy _____   **8.** pretty _____   **9.** steady _____

Add the suffix _-y_ to these words.

10. run _____   **11.** ice _____   **12.** lace _____

Edit and Proofread, continued

Mechanics Workout: Check Abbreviations

Write abbreviations for the words in parentheses.

1. Our teacher, _____ Tennant, helped us with the Welcome! Group.
(Mister)

2. The Welcome! Group is represented by its most important member,

_____ Ahmad Paknejad. **(President)**

3. The conference on the American healthcare system will be presented by

_____ Armstrong. **(Doctor)**

4. _____ Polley has been invited to our school to speak about
immigration laws. **(Senator)**

Check Grammar, Spelling, and Mechanics

**Proofread the passage. Check irregular past tense verbs, words with prefixes
and suffixes, and abbreviations. Correct the mistakes.**

Editing and Proofreading Marks	
∧	Insert something.
∧	Add a comma.
∧	Add a semicolon.
⊙	Add a period.
⊙	Add a colon.
�	Add quotation marks.
⌄	Add apostrophe.
≡	Capitalize.
/	Make lower case.
ℒ	Delete.
¶	Make new paragraph.
◯	Check spelling.
⌒	Replace with this.
∼	Change order.
#	Insert space.
⌒	Close up.

The Welcome! Group beginned its activities yesterday. Pr.
Ahmad Paknejad speaked to the school and letted the new
foreign exchange students introduce themselves. Afterward,
the Welcome! Group haved a big "Merryment Celebration."
Food was plentyful and even Mist. Parker gived the impression
of being in an agreeable mood. The initiative will most likly
be a success.

"I am sure the teachers will see an observeable
improvement from past years," sayed Paknejad. "These foreign
exchange students will speak perfect English by the end of
the semester!"

Edit and Proofread Your Problem-and-Solution Essay

Now edit and proofread your work.

Remember to Check

- ☐ irregular past tense verbs
- ☐ prefixes and suffixes
- ☐ abbreviations
- ☐ _____
- ☐ _____

1. Use a checklist as you edit and proofread. Add things you are working on to the checklist.

2. Look to see which errors are marked most often. Jot down your top three trouble-spots. _____

_____

_____

3. Ask your teacher about ways to fix these mistakes, or check out the Grammar Handbook for information.

Focus on Spelling

Improve your spelling by following these steps.

1. Create a personal spelling list. Record words that you misspelled. Look up correct spelling in the dictionary and add these words to **My Spelling List**.

My Spelling List
funny
believable
disagree
happiness
valuable

2. Pick twelve words. Make each word look interesting and special by tracing it five times. Write the word in one color. Then trace it four more times in four different colors. Say each letter to yourself as you trace it.

3. Work with a partner to play **Spelling Catch**. Pitch words to each other by saying, "Here's the windup. Here's the pitch. The word is . . ." Take turns pitching. The first "batter" to spell ten words correctly wins.

4. Write each spelling word three times. The first time, just write the word. The second time, write it and then circle all the consonants. The third time, write it and circle all the vowels.

5. Play **Memory** to help you remember your words. Write each spelling word on two different index cards. Mix up the cards and place them face down. Turn the cards over two at a time. Your goal is to find the matching cards. Say and spell the words on the cards you turn over. If you make a match, remove those cards from the game. You've won when you've removed all the cards.

Publish, Share, and Reflect

Publish and Share Your Problem-and-Solution Essay

Check the final formats you used to publish your problem-and-solution essay. Then answer the following questions.

Publishing	
What was the final format of your project?	**How did you share your project?**
☐ Wrote it neatly by hand	☐ Shared it with a large group
☐ Typed it on a computer	☐ Shared it with a small group

1. Whether you published it by hand or on the computer, what did you do to dress up your final project?

_____

_____

_____

_____

_____

2. How did you share your work? What did you learn through sharing your work?

_____

_____

_____

_____

_____

_____

_____

_____

_____

_____

_____

_____

Reflect on Your Problem-and-Solution Essay

Read your problem-and-solution essay. Then answer questions 1–6.

1. What do you like best about your work? _____

_____

_____

2. What did you do well? _____

_____

_____

3. What could you improve about your work? _____

_____

_____

_____

4. What did you discover about yourself as you wrote? _____

_____

_____

5. How did your feelings about this issue change as a result of your writing about it?

_____

_____

_____

6. Will you add your problem-and-solution essay to your Writing Portfolio?
Explain your decision.

❑ Yes, I will add this to my Writing Portfolio.

_____

_____

❑ No, I will not add this to my Writing Portfolio.

_____

_____

Analyze a Research Report

What makes this research report a good model?
Read the report and answer the questions.

Lunar Living

by Aria Grishman

In 1969, the first man stepped onto the Moon. In the following three years, another five missions landed men on the Moon. Then, after 1972, the manned missions to the Moon stopped. There has been renewed interest in recent years to further explore the Moon. NASA's goal is to return to the Moon by 2020 (Rios 53). In order to carry out more in-depth experiments and exploration, however, astronauts must be able to stay on the Moon for longer periods. This will require a permanent lunar base. While conditions on the Moon are harsh and inhospitable now, it could be possible to create human settlements there.

The Moon's Environment

The Moon's environment is not suited to human needs. It has almost no atmosphere. Because of this, temperatures can range from 253° Fahrenheit to –388° Fahrenheit (Granger 25). The Moon is also incredibly dry. In fact, "most places on the Moon are so arid that it makes the hottest desert on Earth seem garden-like by comparison" (Whittington 14). In order to live on the Moon, people would need oxygen, water, food, power, and building materials.

Feature Checklist

A good research report

- [ ] is focused on a specific topic
- [ ] gives information from a variety of sources
- [ ] is well organized with an introduction, body, and conclusion.

1. **What does the writer do in the beginning of the report? What is the central idea?**

_____

_____

_____

_____

_____

_____

_____

2. **How many sources does the writer use? How do you know?**

_____

_____

_____

_____

3. **What do you notice about the organization of the report?**

_____

_____

_____

_____

_____

_____

Making the Environment Hospitable

Lunar soil is 43% oxygen (Whittington 49). This oxygen could be processed out of the soil for human use. Certain parts of the Moon also contain hydrogen, which can be combined with oxygen to create water. There are craters near the lunar north and south poles that may have frozen ice crystals in them. These could provide a water source (Whittington 52). Farms could be developed using lamps to provide light during the two-week lunar night (Whittington 77). A small nuclear power station would most likely provide power for settlements. However, solar power could also be used (Whittington 78). Finally, lunar soil could be used to make lunar concrete for building materials (Whittington 64).

Recycling would be even more important for life on the Moon than it is on Earth. Human waste could be used as fertilizer for the farms (Whittington 69). The carbon dioxide that we breathe out would be absorbed by the plants. Then, the plants return oxygen to the air for us to breathe.

Home Sweet Home

The first people to live on the Moon would be scientists, but before long tourists could travel there. Eventually, there could be permanent settlements on the Moon. Moon habitats would be difficult to develop and would be much different than living on Earth, but with modern science and technology, lunar living could become a reality.

4. Why are the headings in the report useful?

_____

_____

_____

_____

_____

_____

5. Is the report focused? Why or why not?

_____

_____

_____

_____

_____

6. How well does the conclusion tie in to the rest of the report? Explain.

_____

_____

_____

_____

_____

_____

_____

© National Geographic Learning, a part of Cengage Learning, Inc.

Plan Your Research

1. List topics about the universe that interest you. Then choose one. Write research questions to pinpoint what you want to know about the topic.

Topic for Discovery	Research Questions

2. Use this diagram to focus your topic and make it specific.

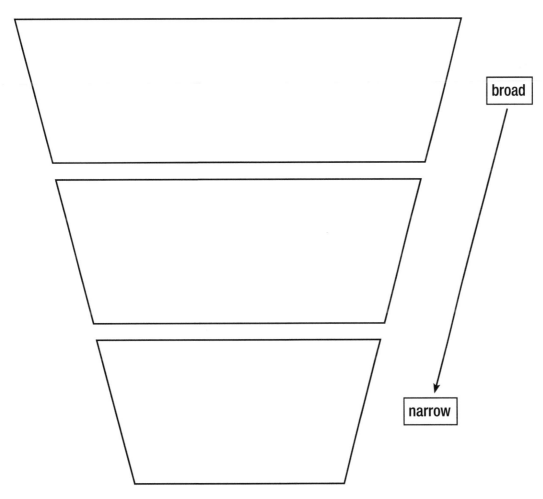

broad

narrow

3. Break down your main research question into more specific questions. Write them on the cards.

Main Question:
_____

Sub–Questions:
_____
_____
_____
_____
_____
_____
_____

Main Question:
_____

Sub–Questions:
_____
_____
_____
_____
_____
_____
_____

Main Question:
_____

Sub–Questions:
_____
_____
_____
_____
_____
_____
_____

Locate Information Sources

A. Brainstorm some ideas for the kinds of information sources you could use for your research report. (You can also jot down ideas from direct observation.)

_____

_____

_____

_____

_____

_____

_____

_____

_____

_____

B. Now list five interview questions you would ask an expert on your topic.

1. _____

_____

_____

2. _____

_____

_____

3. _____

_____

_____

4. _____

_____

_____

5. _____

_____

_____

Locate Information Sources, continued

C. Choose three types of published research sources that would be most helpful in your research. Explain why you chose each information source.

Type of Source: _____

_____

_____

Type of Source: _____

_____

_____

Type of Source: _____

_____

_____

D. Use an online catalog to search for print and multimedia resources. List the title (and author, if possible) of each source.

1. _____

_____

2. _____

_____

3. _____

_____

4. _____

_____

E. List four Web sites that you think will be helpful for writing your research report. Make sure you choose reputable Web sites you can trust.

1. _____

2. _____

3. _____

4. _____

© National Geographic Learning, a part of Cengage Learning, Inc.

Get Information from the Web

A. Describe or name any databases you used. List titles and summaries of any useful articles you found on each database.

1. _____
_____
_____
_____

2. _____
_____
_____
_____

3. _____
_____
_____
_____

B. What search engines did you use? List titles and summaries of any useful articles you found through a search engine. If possible, include the Web site address.

1. _____
_____
_____

Web site Address: _____

2. _____
_____
_____

Web site Address: _____

3. _____
_____
_____

Web site Address: _____

Evaluate Sources

A. Look at these print sources. Then answer the questions.

People last set foot on the Moon more than 35 years ago. However, NASA has announced plans to not only go back to the Moon, but to stay there. NASA is planning to build a permanent lunar base by the year 2020. Atmospheric conditions on the Moon make the environment hostile to human life. But astronauts can use materials found in the lunar soil to survive. Oxygen and hydrogen can be found near the lunar poles. These locations also give astronauts access to large amounts of sunlight. This will allow them to use solar power to fuel the base.

—BY DONOVAN RICE, Ph.D.

from *Riverdale Gazette*, November 2007

Dr. Rice is part of the NASA team developing future lunar habitats.

Just think. Someday we may be living on the Moon! NASA has announced that they are considering building a permanent settlement on the Moon. They believe there might be enough natural resources in the soil on the Moon to use. Many scientists believe the north and south poles on the Moon will be good places to set up a base. The decision will be made final in the next couple of years.

—BY MARIA OLIVARA

from *Mendenhall Middle School Times*, April 2004

Maria Olivara is in the eighth grade at Mendenhall Middle School.

1. Which source is more likely to contain up-to-date-information? Why?

_____

_____

2. What is the purpose of each print source? Explain your answer.

_____

_____

3. Which source is more likely to be accurate and reliable? Explain your answer.

_____

_____

Evaluate Sources, continued

B. Look at the two Web sites. Then answer the questions on page 96.

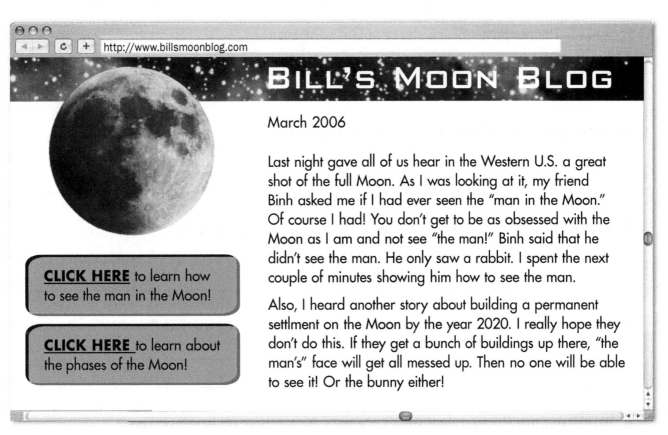

http://www.billsmoonblog.com

BILL'S MOON BLOG

March 2006

Last night gave all of us hear in the Western U.S. a great shot of the full Moon. As I was looking at it, my friend Binh asked me if I had ever seen the "man in the Moon." Of course I had! You don't get to be as obsessed with the Moon as I am and not see "the man!" Binh said that he didn't see the man. He only saw a rabbit. I spent the next couple of minutes showing him how to see the man.

Also, I heard another story about building a permanent settlment on the Moon by the year 2020. I really hope they don't do this. If they get a bunch of buildings up there, "the man's" face will get all messed up. Then no one will be able to see it! Or the bunny either!

CLICK HERE to learn how to see the man in the Moon!

CLICK HERE to learn about the phases of the Moon!

http://www.sciencetoday.edu

Science Today

Moon Base No Longer Science Fiction
By Laila Gillani, Ph.D.
April 2008

NASA scientists are developing plans for a permanent base on the Moon. The base wouldn't be complete until 2020. However, teams have begun solving the problems that a base would encounter. The main problem is sustainability. How would astronauts find the resources to live? Methods are being developed that would allow humans to use the lunar soil and landscape to sustain life.

The main obstacle is the lack of oxygen in non-Earth environments. However, new techniques have been developed that would allow oxygen to be extracted from the lunar soil. Once a lunar farm is created, plants could also contribute to the base's oxygen supply.

See also: Lunar Life, *U.S. Journal of Space*, March 2008

C. Use the two Web sites on page 95 to answer the questions.

1. What is the purpose of each site? Explain your answer.

_____

_____

2. Who wrote the material that appears on each site?

_____

_____

3. Which of the two Web sites contains more up-to-date information?

_____

_____

4. How could you check to see if the facts on the first Web site are true?

_____

_____

5. Would you use the first Web site as a source for a report on living on the Moon? Why or why not?

_____

_____

6. Which of the two Web sites looks more professional? Explain your answer.

_____

_____

7. Based on the two sites' URLs, which site is more reliable? Why?

_____

_____

8. Choose one of the two Web sites, and list two facts from the site that you think could be used in a report.

_____

_____

_____

Locate Relevant Information

Skim and scan this magazine article. Then answer the questions.

Intelligent Life on the Moon: Past, Present, and Future

Historic Beliefs and Theories

Some primitive cultures believed that the Moon itself was a powerful god or supernatural force. Others believed that their ancestors came from the Moon.

Several ancient western philosophers, including Anaxagoras and Xenophanes, believed that intelligent life might exist on the Moon.

Following the studies of astronomers Copernicus and Galileo, scientists grew more interested in the possibility of lunar life.

Galileo was the first to view the moon through a telescope. Scientists studied the images through the telescope, and some saw evidence of life.

Robots Pave Way for Lunar Life

Space probes are already collecting data about the Moon. Other unmanned craft, such as robotic landers and rovers, may be sent to study the surface further. Why all this research? Scientists hope to someday have human settlements on the Moon. Robotic craft will collect the data scientists need to build life support systems. First, a structure that can be visited by astronauts will be built. Eventually, scientists plan to build a structure that will house a permanent human colony.

1. Read the title. Does it tell you that this article might be useful to someone writing about plans for a human colony on the Moon? Explain.

_____

_____

_____

_____

_____

_____

2. Which part of the article would you read first to look for information about a human colony on the Moon? Why?

_____

_____

_____

_____

3. Which information is useful to someone writing about plans for a human colony on the Moon? Which information is not useful?

_____

_____

_____

_____

_____

_____

_____

Take Good Notes

A. Read the excerpt from the article. Then answer the questions.

Space Food   41

By Bryan Bertson

One of the challenges astronauts face in the zero-gravity of space is
how and what to eat.

The situation has definitely improved over time. Early astronauts had
to eat bite-sized cubes that crumbled everywhere, freeze-dried powders,
and goo squeezed out of tubes. Many astronauts complained about their
food.

Modern astronauts have more to choose from. Some foods, like
brownies and fruit, can be eaten as is. Other food, such as spaghetti,
must be rehydrated. You have to add water to it to eat it. There is even
salt and pepper available, although it is in liquid form. If you sprinkled it,
it would just float away! It might clog vents, damage machinery, or get in
astronauts' eyes, mouths, or throats.

1. Why should you take notes when you read or research a topic?

_____

2. What should you do to show that you are using exact words from a source?

_____

3. Why should you take note of the author, title, and page number of a source?

_____

4. After reading this article, what information would you record so that you
can later find the article easily?

_____

5. What is one important fact from the article you would record in your notes?

_____

Take Good Notes, continued

B. Now use these index cards to take notes on the excerpt from page 98.

<u>Space Food—Then</u>
—
—

<u>Space Food—Now</u>
—
—

—

Paraphrasing

Read the source material.
Then paraphrase the important ideas.

At a Glance

To paraphrase:

• read the source carefully

• record the important information in your own words

• keep your paraphrase the same length as the original or a bit shorter.

Space Laundry
By Kevin Pastor

Did you know that space station crews do not change clothes every day? They bring a limited amount of clothing to space. They get one pair of shorts and one T-shirt for every three days of exercising. They get one work shirt and pair of shorts or pants for every ten days of work! They change their underwear and socks every other day. This may seem awful, but the crews don't get as dirty in space as we do on Earth!

Astronaut's Clothing

Incredible Suits!
By Laura Corty

Have you ever seen the orange suits worn by astronauts? Those are called Launch and Entry Suits (LES), and they are amazing! Each suit is designed to maintain air pressure if the shuttle cabin were to leak. They also have equipment for emergency landings.

Each suit contains parachutes, a radio, and drinking water. There is also a beacon to alert rescuers. In case of a water landing, the suits have insulation. It's amazing the astronauts can still walk around with all that stuff in their clothes!

Astronaut's Clothing

Take Good Notes, continued

Summarizing

1. Read the article carefully. Then summarize it.

Relaxing and Sleeping in Space

Toya Jackson

When you are not working, chances are you're either relaxing and having fun or sleeping. The same goes for astronauts aboard the International Space Station. It is important for astronauts to take a break from work and relax every now and then.

There are many things astronauts can do to relax and have fun. One of the easiest things to do is to just look out the window. They might look at Earth, or they might gaze into the inky blackness of space. The crew can also read books, play cards, or joke around with each other. Astronauts must take some time to exercise each day. Crew members can strap themselves into a treadmill or exercise bike and work out.

There are many sleeping options, too. Early astronauts slept in their command chairs. Now, astronauts can sleep in sleeping bags that act like cocoons, in bunk beds, or by tying themselves to a wall. When there's no gravity, you can sleep vertically!

56

Summary:

_____

_____

_____

_____

_____

_____

2. Now that you know about note taking, create your own index cards. Use them to take notes on the sources you have decided to use for your research report.

Avoid Plagiarism

Read the source and the student paper. Then edit the student paper to fix any plagiarism.

At a Glance

To avoid accidental plagiarism:

- use quotation marks around any text taken directly from a source
- use your own wording and sentence patterns when paraphrasing ideas
- give credit to the writer (or source) whenever you quote or paraphrase another writer's ideas.

Source

Colonization Prospects
Judith Rukowski

Many scientists are searching for an acceptable location for human colonization. The two best candidates so far are our Moon and the planet Mars. There are both benefits and drawbacks to each location. Conditions, resources, and economics must all be considered.

Both places have elements that would support human habitation. The Moon has oxygen in its soil. This oxygen could be mined for human use. Mars has large amounts of CO_2 in its thin atmosphere. This would be useful for plant growth, which would in turn naturally provide oxygen.

63

Student Paper

Moon vs. Mars

Many factors are important when considering whether to colonize the Moon or Mars. Conditions, resources, and economics should be evaluated. Each location has its own benefits and drawbacks.

Both sites have the potential for oxygen, which is necessary for human life. "The Moon has oxygen in its soil. It could be removed with modern technology. Mars's atmosphere has CO_2 that would help plant growth. The plants could produce oxygen for humans to breathe.

Using Direct Quotes

1. On each index card, record an important quote from the article. Use ellipses or brackets as needed.

At a Glance

Follow these tips when you use a direct quote:

- copy the words exactly
- use brackets [ ] around any words you changed
- use ellipses (...) to show where you left words out.

Settling on the Moon, or Mars?

By Noble Taylor

Many scientists believe that we don't have a choice between colonizing the Moon or Mars first. The Moon may not be the best long-term location. But it would be cheaper and easier to start there.

Colonizing the Moon first could give us practice for living on Mars. On the Moon, scientists could develop the technology needed to give colonists the best habitats for living in a new, hostile environment.

Also, it would take less fuel to travel from Earth to the Moon than to Mars. If something goes wrong during a spaceflight between the Moon and Earth there would be enough time for a shuttle to get help. On a flight to Mars, it would be nearly impossible to rescue a shuttle in trouble.

Most scientists agree that humans should colonize the Moon first. What we learn about living on the Moon could make living on Mars better and easier.

2. Record one good quote you plan to use in your research report.

_____

_____

_____

_____

_____

_____

First Colonies—the Moon or Mars

"On the Moon, scientists could develop the technology . . . for living in a new, hostile environment."

Taylor, 8

First Colonies—the Moon or Mars

First Colonies—the Moon or Mars

First Colonies—the Moon or Mars

Synthesizing Ideas

Study the Inquiry Chart. Then write a synthesis of the information presented for each research question.

Research Questions	Source Information	Synthesis
Why was the space shuttle program conceived?	There was a need to find a spacecraft that was reusable. (Zhou 60) NASA had designs for a space shuttle prior to the Apollo moon landing. (Harvey 52) The Department of Defense was an early supporter of the space shuttle program. (O'Hanley 32)	
Were there any obstacles in the way of the Space Shuttle program?	The NASA budget was reduced by a billion dollars. (Rogers 34) Both houses of Congress were skeptical about an expanded space program. (Anderson 101) Critics of the program were constantly forcing NASA to cut costs. (Ramirez 111)	

Check for Focus

**Delete any information that doesn't relate to the research question.
Then write a synthesis of the information.**

Research Questions	Source Information	Synthesis
How can a solar eclipse be harmful to the eyes?	Intense radiation that emits from the sun's photosphere can permanently damage the retina. (White 25)	_____
		_____
	In 2002, more than 40,000 eye-related injuries were reported in the United States. (Harris 33)	_____
		_____
	Looking at an eclipse through optical aids like telescopes can cause thermal burning of the retinas. (Kurtz 32)	_____
		_____
	Solar eclipses occur every year, but total eclipses are still considered rare. (Rayman 27)	_____
		_____
	While staring at the sun is always dangerous, eclipses cause people to gaze longer. (Arenas 52)	_____
		_____
	The sun can only be viewed directly if specially designed filters are used. (Campbell 84)	_____

Develop an Outline

1. Write a draft of your outline for your research report:

- **use roman numerals for the main topics in your paper**
- **use capital letters for ideas that will become the main ideas in your paragraphs**
- **use numbers for details.**

_____

_____

_____

_____

_____

_____

_____

_____

_____

_____

_____

_____

_____

_____

_____

_____

_____

_____

_____

_____

_____

_____

_____

_____

Develop an Outline, continued

2. Now type your outline with correct indentation and paste it here.

Draft a Research Report

1. Use the outline to draft an introductory paragraph for this report.

> **I. Introduction**
>
>   A. Soviet Union successfully launched Sputnik 1 satellite in the 1950s
>
>   B. Was determined to send an animal into orbit next
>
>   C. Had political motive for sending another satellite

_____

_____

_____

_____

_____

_____

_____

2. Use your outline from pages 106–107 to draft an introductory paragraph for your research report.

_____

_____

_____

_____

_____

_____

_____

_____

_____

_____

_____

_____

_____

_____

Draft a Research Report, continued

3. Use the outline to draft a body paragraph for this report.

> **II. Finding Laika**
>
> A. Laika was one of three dogs selected for the program
>
> B. A former stray on the streets of Moscow
>
> C. Dogs trained on rockets and tested life support systems

_____

_____

_____

_____

_____

_____

_____

_____

4. Use your outline from pages 106–107 to draft a body paragraph for your research report.

_____

_____

_____

_____

_____

_____

_____

_____

_____

_____

_____

_____

_____

_____

_____

_____

5. Use the outline to draft a concluding paragraph for this report.

> **V. Conclusion**
>
> A. Laika launched into space on November 3, 1957
>
> B. Did not survive the mission and died after a few days
>
> C. Allowed scientists to understand how living organisms behave in space

_____

_____

_____

_____

_____

_____

_____

6. Use your outline from pages 106–107 to draft a concluding paragraph for your research report.

_____

_____

_____

_____

_____

_____

_____

_____

_____

_____

_____

_____

_____

Name _____ Date _____

Make Source Cards

Locate sources for your report. Record the information here for the sources you used. List the details you need for each type.

Source Card

Source #1
Type: Book
Title:
Author:
Publisher:
City:
Year:

Note Card

Source Card

Source #2
Type:
Title:
Author:

Note Card

Source Card

Source #3
Type:
Title:
Author:

Note Card

Source Card

Source #4
Type:
Title:
Author:

Note Card

Create a List of Works Cited

Create a list of works cited for your research report. Include all the sources you quoted or that you paraphrased. Look on page 197W of your book if you need help.

Works Cited

_____

_____

_____

_____

_____

_____

_____

_____

_____

_____

_____

_____

_____

_____

_____

_____

_____

_____

_____

_____

_____

_____

_____

_____

_____

_____

_____

_____

Revise a Research Report

1. Use the checklist. Evaluate this draft of the beginning of a research report. What changes are needed?

_____

_____

_____

_____

Revising Checklist

- ☐ Is my introduction interesting?
- ☐ Does my paper have a clear central idea?
- ☐ Are there any unrelated details that should be taken out?
- ☐ Are the sentences in the most logical order?

2. Revise the draft. Use revising marks to show your changes.

Revising

MARK	WHAT IT MEANS
∧	Insert something.
↶	Move to here.
∧‾	Replace with this.
⟋	Take out.
¶	Make a new paragraph.

Land of the Midnight Sun

The midnight sun occurs within the Arctic Circle and the Antarctic Circle (Harlen 107). Alaska is the only place in the United States with a midnight sun. Alaska is farther away from the North Pole. So it gets only one full day of sunlight per year. This makes it hard for people to sleep.

This happens because of the way the Earth's axis is tilted. This angle keeps the North Pole facing the sun all summer. It tilts at about 23 degrees (Springer 42). Alaska is located close enough to the North Pole to get one day of 24-hour sunlight per year.

3. Now use the checklist to help you revise the draft of your research report.

Edit and Proofread

Grammar Workout:
Check Subject and Object Pronouns

Use pronouns from the box to complete each sentence.
Then circle the word each pronoun replaces.

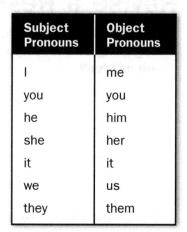

Subject Pronouns	Object Pronouns
I	me
you	you
he	him
she	her
it	it
we	us
they	them

1. When meteorites hit, _____ create large holes in the ground.

2. The crater can be so large that you can't see the other side of _____ .

3. Gilbert studied the craters on the Moon. _____ wanted to know if _____ were made by meteors.

4. I would like to study impact craters. _____ have always fascinated _____ .

Spelling Workout: Check Silent Consonants

Use proofreader's marks to correct mistakes in the following sentences.

1. Gilbert studied the Moon in the knight sky.

2. Gilbert wanted to no how the craters on the Moon formed.

3. He douted that they were formed by volcanic eruptions.

4. Gilbert's theory that the craters were the result of meteor impacts was write.

5. The scientists who thought the craters were caused by volcanoes were rong.

Edit and Proofread, continued

Mechanics Workout: Check Punctuation and Capitalization of Sources

Use proofreading marks to correct the following citations.

1. Whittington, Mark. living on the moon." *Associated Content.* 29 Nov. 2005. 21 Mar. 2008. <www.associatedcontent.com/article/11893/livingonmoon.html>.

2. Bordeaux, melvin. *Adapting to Space.* Boston; Random House, 2006

3. Chen, Joyce "Home, Home On the Moon." *Science Weekly.* 7 Nov. 2007: 42.

4. Smith Lana. "Extreme Temperatures on the Moon." *Science Weekly.* 14 Oct 2006.

Check Grammar, Spelling, and Mechanics

Proofread the passage. Check subject and object pronouns, silent consonants, and the punctuation and capitalization of citations. Correct the mistakes.

Editing and Proofreading Marks	
∧	Insert something.
⋏	Add a comma.
⋏	Add a semicolon.
⊙	Add a period.
⊙	Add a colon.
✌ ✌	Add quotation marks.
✌	Add apostrophe.
≡	Capitalize.
/	Make lower case.
℘	Delete.
¶	Make new paragraph.
◯	Spell out.
⌐	Replace with this.
∩	Change order.
#	Insert space.
◡	Close up.

Once sientists new that the moon craters were caused by meteors, them were able to figure out some things about Earth, too. They found a large crater in Arizona. Scientists douted that he was formed by a volcano. Based on knew nowledge about moon craters, scientists decided that this crater was also formed by a meteor. It is now nown as "Meteor Crater."

Chicxulub Crater is another large crater in Mexico. Many scientists believe this meteor crash killed the dinosaurs! Don't get fooled by Crater Lake in Oregon, though. They really was the result of a volcano!

daigle, Kelly. *Earth's Craters*, Austin Phoenix Books, 2003

Edit and Proofread Your Research Report

Now edit and proofread your work.

1. Use a checklist as you edit and proofread. Add things you are working on to the checklist.

2. Look to see which errors are marked most often. Jot down your top three trouble spots.

_____

_____

_____

3. Ask your teacher about ways to fix these mistakes, or check out the Grammar Handbook for information.

Focus on Spelling

Improve your spelling by following these steps.

My Spelling List
knight
wrench
kneel
wrong
know

1. Create a personal spelling list. Record words that you misspelled. Look up correct spelling in the dictionary and add these words to **My Spelling List**.

2. Pick twelve words. Focus on four words each day. Write your words before each meal and check the spelling. At the end of the week, try writing all twelve words.

3. Play **Spelling Behind Your Back**. Have your partner stand with his or her back to the board. List your partner's spelling words on the board. Say each word and ask your partner to spell it. Switch roles.

4. Organize your words into different lists. List your words from shortest word to longest word. Next list them from easiest to hardest. Then try listing them in reverse alphabetical order.

5. Invent your own acronyms. Think of a word that begins with each letter. The words in the correct order should be easy for you to remember. For example:

Spelling word	**Acronym**
ocean	**o**ctopus, **c**oral, **e**el, **a**re, near

Publish, Share, and Reflect

Publish and Share Your Research Report

**Check the final formats you used to publish your research report.
Then answer the following questions.**

Publishing

What was the final format of your project?	How did you share your project?
☐ Wrote it neatly by hand	☐ Shared it with a large group
☐ Typed it on a computer	☐ Shared it with a small group

1. Whether you published it by hand or on the computer, what did you do to dress up your final project?

_____

_____

_____

_____

_____

2. How did you share your work? What did you learn through sharing your work?

_____

_____

_____

_____

_____

_____

_____

_____

_____

_____

_____

_____

_____

Reflect on Your Research

Reflect on the process you used to research your report.
Write the title of your report here: _____

Gathering Information

1. What did you do that helped you gather information for your report?

_____

_____

2. What will you do differently when you gather information for your next report?

_____

_____

Organizing and Digesting Information

3. What did you do that helped you organize and digest information for your report?

_____

_____

_____

4. What will you do differently when you organize and digest information for your next report?

_____

_____

Presenting Information

5. What did you do that helped you present information in your report?

_____

_____

6. What will you do differently when you present information in your next report?

_____

_____

Analyze a Narrative Poem

What makes this poem a good model? Read the poem and answer the questions.

© National Geographic Learning, a part of Cengage Learning, Inc.

Feature Checklist

A good narrative poem

☐ focuses on one topic or event

☐ may express feelings about the event

☐ can have a narrator and characters

☐ uses precise words and sensory language to tell about the event.

Fluttering Away

by Kate Latham

There it was
on the bench,
opening and
closing itself
like the book
it distracted me from reading.
Its sunset wings
with spider-leg lines
and drops of white
doubled as it opened,
then shrank back.
I must have moved
because,
to my sigh,
it fluttered away.

Another monarch
will take my windowsill
for its throne.
Maybe another
will rule over the front stoop
and my attention.
But what if that's it?
What if,
three or four or twenty visits from now,
all the monarchs
flutter away?

1. What image is the focus of the poem?

_____

_____

_____

2. What feelings does the poet express?

_____

_____

_____

3. Give two examples of colorful language from the poem.

_____

_____

_____

3. What makes this poem a free-verse poem?

_____

_____

_____

Plan a Narrative Poem

Use page 120 to plan your poem.

1. Choose a topic or an event that you're passionate about. Use the diagram below to narrow down your topic.

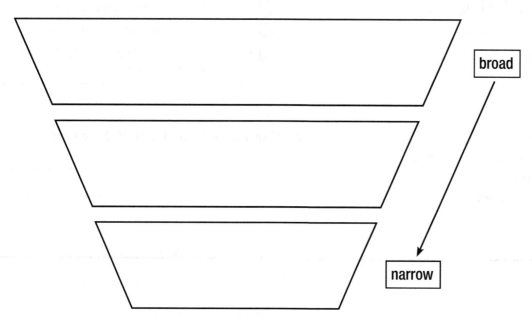

2. Jot down ideas and impressions about your topic or event. Include words, phrases, and drawings that you associate with your topic.

Draft a Narrative Poem

Use your plan from page 120 to write the first draft of your poem.

Drafting Checklist

☐ Focus on a single subject, image, or event.

☐ Express your feelings about your subject.

☐ Use vivid, precise, and colorful language.

☐ Include a narrator and characters if you wish.

Revise a Narrative Poem

1. Use the checklist to evaluate this draft of a narrative poem in free verse. What changes are needed?

_____

_____

_____

_____

_____

_____

Revising Checklist

- ☐ Is the poem focused on one topic or event? Is the image well developed?
- ☐ Is it clear how the poet feels about the topic?
- ☐ Are there enough vivid details to keep the reader engaged?
- ☐ Does the poet use precise words and sensory language to tell about the event?

2. Revise this draft. Use revising marks to show your changes.

Revising

MARK	WHAT IT MEANS
∧	Insert something.
⌒	Move to here.
⌢	Replace with this.
◞	Take out.
¶	Make a new paragraph.

In the Bamboo Forests

On a snowy mountain in China,

a panda forages for bamboo.

Bamboo is the main source of a panda's diet.

In the cold, its black and white fur looks

like it would make a warm blanket.

Its other features make the panda

look like a toy bear has come to life!

Childlike, it crawls—mischief in its black-rimmed eyes—

looking for a nice, comfortable spot to rest.

With a bunch of bamboo in its hands

the panda gets ready for a tasty meal

3. Now use the checklist to help you revise the draft of your narrative poem in free verse on page 121.

© National Geographic Learning, a part of Cengage Learning, Inc.

Edit and Proofread

Grammar Workout: Check Descriptive Adjectives

Use a caret to add a descriptive adjective to each sentence.

1. A chimpanzee raced toward a tree.

2. He grasped the trunk with his arms.

3. He scampered up the tree, and then stopped to sit on a branch.

4. His chatter made me cover my ears.

5. Then the chimp beat his chest with his fists.

6. I watched the chimp swing on the branch for minutes.

7. Then he dropped to the ground and turned his face toward me.

8. I had to laugh at his attitude.

Spelling Workout: Check Suffixes in Verbs Ending in y

Add the -ed ending to each verb.

1. dry _____   **3.** stay _____   **5.** spy _____

2. convey _____   **4.** try _____   **6.** annoy _____

Add the -ing ending to each verb.

7. pry _____   **9.** rely _____   **11.** fly _____

8. carry _____   **10.** deny _____   **12.** simplify _____

Mechanics Workout: Check Punctuation

Add punctuation where you think it belongs. Delete any confusing punctuation.

Saving the Elephant

An African elephant can have

Its two tusks

Four legs.

Swamps bushlands

Three hundred, pounds of food per day

Sixty years of life

An African elephant can have,

All these things

If we let him

Check Grammar, Spelling, and Mechanics

Proofread the poem. Check the spelling and punctuation. Correct the mistakes, and add descriptive adjectives where you can.

Editing and Proofreading Marks	
∧	Insert something.
⌃	Add a comma.
⌃	Add a semicolon.
⊙	Add a period.
⊙	Add a colon.
⌄ ⌄	Add quotation marks.
⌄	Add apostrophe.
≡	Capitalize.
/	Make lower case.
℘	Delete.
¶	Make new paragraph.
◯	Check spelling.
⌒	Replace with this.
∼	Change order.
#	Insert space.
⌒	Close up.

The Leatherback

One flip, at a time

Of her front flippers

The, leatherback turtle

Tryed

To get to shore

Now finally she can rest

Liing on the beach

Laiing her eggs

Edit and Proofread, continued

Edit and Proofread Your Poem

Now edit and proofread your work.

1. Use a checklist as you edit and proofread. Add things you are working on to the checklist.

2. Look to see which errors are marked most often. Jot down your top three trouble spots.

_____

_____

_____

3. Ask your teacher about ways to fix these mistakes, or check out the Grammar Handbook for information.

Focus on Spelling

Improve your spelling by following these steps.

1. Create a personal spelling list. Record words that you misspelled. Look up correct spelling in the dictionary and add these words to **My Spelling List**.

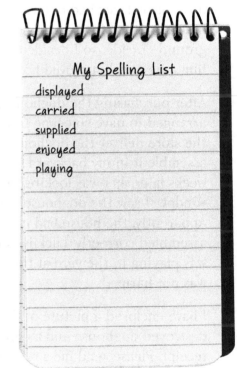

My Spelling List
displayed
carried
supplied
enjoyed
playing

2. Pick twelve words. Make a colorful display of the words. Get a sheet of chart paper. Write each word three times in a different color.

3. Work with a partner to play **Spelling Tic-Tac-Toe**. Draw a tic-tac-toe board. Take turns asking each other to spell words. When a player spells a word correctly, that player gets to mark an X or an O on the game board.

4. Write the letters for each word on separate squares of paper. Attach the letters for each word to each other with a paper clip. Unscramble the letters to spell each of your words.

5. Invent your own memory strategy for difficult words. Think of a good way to remember *why* letters appear (or not) in a word. For example:

Word	**Explanation**
dessert	"It has two s's for **s**weet **s**tuff!"

Analyze a Business Letter

What makes this business letter a good model?
Read the letter and answer the questions.

321 Hammond Avenue
San José, CA 95113
May 22, 2014

Alicia Ortega
District Manager
Pads for Pets
53 Lawson Road
San José, CA 95113

Dear Ms. Ortega:

On May 6, 2014, I visited your store and purchased a doghouse for my dog, Tiger. Tiger had outgrown his old house and had been sleeping on the ground outside, so I decided to buy him a new and improved home.

After purchasing the doghouse, I arranged to have someone from the store deliver the doghouse and assemble it in my backyard. Two weeks later, as I was looking out the window, I saw the doghouse collapse. Apparently, the house had not been assembled correctly. Luckily, my dog was playing in the yard at the time and was not harmed.

I have enclosed a picture of the destroyed doghouse and a copy of my receipt. Please send me a refund for my purchase. Feel free to contact me by phone at (555) 894-9954 if you need to speak with me. Thank you for your quick response to this matter.

Sincerely,
Jonathan Palmer
Jonathan Palmer

1. **What is the writer's purpose for writing?**

_____

_____

_____

_____

2. **What evidence does the writer provide that proves the doghouse was not assembled correctly?**

_____

_____

_____

_____

3. **What tone does the writer use? How can you tell?**

_____

_____

_____

_____

_____

_____

_____

_____

_____

_____

© National Geographic Learning, a part of Cengage Learning, Inc.

Plan a Business Letter

Use pages 127–128 to plan your business letter.

1. Plan what you'll say about the problem. Answer each question in this list.

Question	Answer
What did I buy?	_____
	_____
	_____
When did I buy it?	_____
	_____
	_____
Where did I buy it?	_____
	_____
	_____
What was the problem?	_____
	_____
	_____
Why was it a problem?	_____
	_____
	_____

2. Use the phone, Internet, or other resources to find out whom to contact about the problem. Write down that person's name, address, and any other important contact information.

Name of contact: _____

Address: _____

_____

_____

Other information: _____

_____

3. Make a list of possible solutions to your problem. Then, decide on the solution you want. Circle the solution you choose.

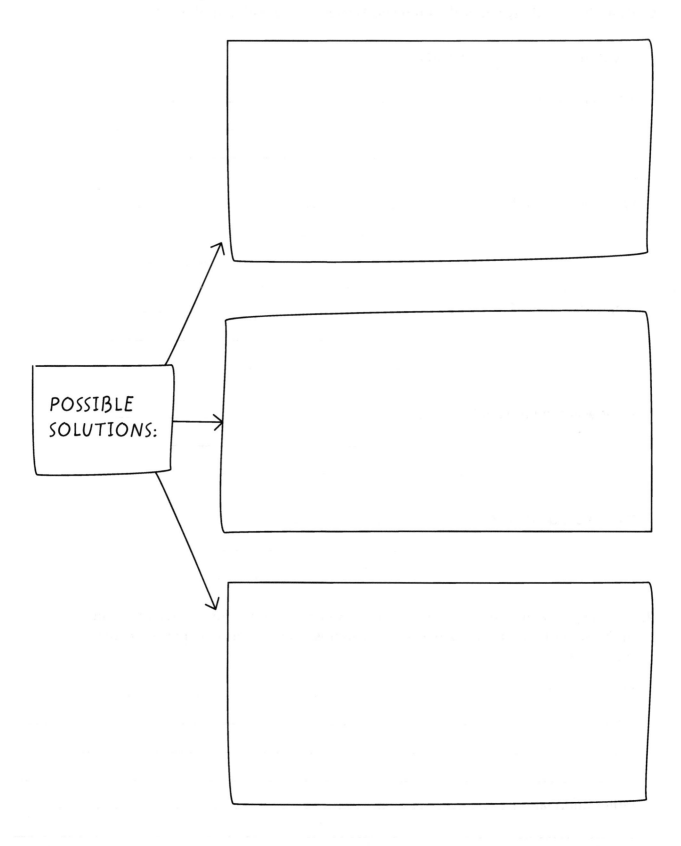

Draft a Business Letter

Use your plan from pages 127–128 to write the first draft of your business letter.

Drafting Checklist

☐ Include your address and the date, and the recipient's name and address.

☐ Use a formal greeting.

☐ State the problem clearly and suggest a solution. Make a claim and give evidence for why the solution you suggest is a fair one.

☐ Use a formal and polite tone.

☐ End with a formal closing and your signature.

_____

_____

_____

_____

_____

_____

_____

_____

_____

_____

_____

_____

_____

_____

_____

_____

_____

_____

_____

_____

Revise a Business Letter

1. Use the checklist to evaluate this part of a draft for a business letter. What changes are needed?

_____

_____

_____

_____

_____

2. Revise this draft. Use revising marks to show your changes.

MARK	WHAT IT MEANS
∧	Insert something.
↶	Move to here.
∧—	Replace with this.
___ℯ	Take out.
¶	Make a new paragraph.

I am writing to you about a damaged CD. The CD is called Whale Songs. I bought this CD at the Ferndale Aquarium gift shop.

On my class trip to the aquarium last week, I visited the gift shop and bought Whale Songs. When I got home and opened the box, I discovered a huge scratch on the back of the disc. I put the disc in my CD player, but it refused to play.

Please send me a new copy of Whale Songs as a replacement for the damaged CD. I am enclosing the damaged CD. I am also sending you my receipt from the gift shop.

3. Now use the checklist to help you revise the draft of your business letter on page 129.

Name _____ Date _____

Edit and Proofread

Grammar Workout: Check Comparative Adjectives

Add -er or more to the adjective in parentheses. Write the new comparative adjective in the sentence.

1. I knew I wanted a camera that would last _____ than my old camera. **(long)**

2. My old camera is shiny and _____ than either of the new cameras I looked at. **(stylish)**

3. Both of the new cameras were _____ than the old one. **(powerful)**

4. I asked the sales clerk which camera was a _____ product. **(popular)**

5. She said the Sharper Shot camera would be a _____ choice for me. **(smart)**

Spelling Workout: Check Adjectives Ending in -er and -est

Add the suffix -er to these words.

1. wet _____   **3.** late _____   **5.** silly _____

2. happy _____   **4.** thin _____   **6.** blue _____

Add the suffix -est to these words.

7. red _____   **9.** pure _____   **11.** scary _____

8. heavy _____   **10.** nice _____   **12.** sad _____

Mechanics Workout: Check Capitalization and Punctuation

Proofread this part of a business letter. Fix the capitalization and punctuation errors.

dear Mr. guttierez

In your magazine's June issue, you reported that the Sharper Shot camera took the best pictures. However, I used a Sharper Shot and all the pictures were blurry. Can you perform more tests on it? Thank you for considering my suggestion.

sincerely

Ellen Brooks

Check Grammar, Spelling, and Mechanics

Proofread the letter. Check the spelling, the capitalization and punctuation, and the use of comparative adjectives. Correct the mistakes.

Editing and Proofreading Marks	
∧	Insert something.
⋏	Add a comma.
⊹	Add a semicolon.
⊙	Add a period.
⊙	Add a colon.
⌄⌄	Add quotation marks.
⌄	Add apostrophe.
≡	Capitalize.
/	Make lower case.
℘	Delete.
¶	Make new paragraph.
◯	Check spelling.
⌒	Replace with this.
∾	Change order.
#	Insert space.
◡	Close up.

Mr. samuel resnick

Sharper Shot Camera Co.

6312 Circle Court

Springfield, IL 62701

dear Mr. resnick

Thank you for the new camera. It is the niceest camera I have ever used. I was able to take professionaler pictures with it than I was with the first one. I am now your company's big fan. I will tell my friends that Sharper Shot Camera Co. is enjoyabler to work with than any other company!

regards

Ellen Brooks

© National Geographic Learning, a part of Cengage Learning, Inc.

Edit and Proofread, continued

Edit and Proofread Your Business Letter

Now edit and proofread your work.

1. Use a checklist as you edit and proofread. Add things you are working on to the checklist.

2. Look to see which errors are marked most often. Jot down your top three trouble-spots.

_____

_____

_____

3. Ask your teacher about ways to fix these mistakes, or check out the Grammar Handbook for information.

Focus on Spelling

Improve your spelling by following these steps.

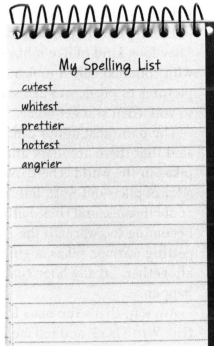

1. Create a personal spelling list. Record words that you misspelled. Look up correct spelling in the dictionary and add these words to **My Spelling List**.

2. Pick twelve words. Write six sentences, using two of the words in each sentence. Wacky sentences are just fine! Double-check the spelling. Then write six different sentences, using different pairs of spelling words.

3. Organize your words into different lists. List your words in alphabetical order. Next list them from shortest word to longest. Spell the words aloud as you write them.

4. Make a personal word wall with your spelling words. List your words on chart paper. Read the words on your word wall. Then spell them letter by letter. Next close your eyes and spell them again, letter by letter. Open your eyes. Did you spell the word correctly?

5. Invent a story to help you remember difficult words. For example:
Word: cemetery

Story: I got scared walking through the cemetery and yelled, "e-e-e!" as I ran away.
(The word *cemetery* has three e's.)

Analyze a Friendly Letter

What makes this friendly letter a good model?
Read the letter and answer the questions.

Feature Checklist

A good friendly letter

- ☐ begins with the date in the upper right corner
- ☐ includes a greeting
- ☐ uses an informal tone to tell about recent events and about the writer's thoughts and feelings
- ☐ asks about your friend's life
- ☐ includes a closing before the signature.

1. **How do the first two lines of Marcus's letter follow the format of a friendly letter?**

_____

_____

_____

2. **What kind of tone does Marcus use? How can you tell?**

_____

_____

_____

_____

3. **How does Marcus show interest in Drew's life?**

_____

_____

_____

_____

4. **What closing does Marcus use? Could he use this closing in a business letter?**

_____

_____

_____

_____

Plan a Friendly Letter

Use pages 135–136 to plan your friendly letter.

1. List several interesting or exciting things you have done recently. Then choose one to write about.

Ideas

- _____
- _____
- _____

2. Plan how your ideas will flow. Use a graphic organizer to put your central idea and details in order.

Central Idea

Detail 1

Detail 2

Detail 3

3. Which style of voice is best for you? Try each style. Then choose the style you'll use for your letter.

STYLE	EXAMPLE
Cheerful	
Informative	
Affectionate	
Concerned	
Hopeful	

Draft a Friendly Letter

Use your plan from pages 135–136 to write the first draft of your friendly letter.

Drafting Checklist

- ☐ Begin with the date in the upper right corner.
- ☐ Include a greeting.
- ☐ Use an informal tone.
- ☐ Tell about an event or experience, and include your thoughts and feelings.
- ☐ Ask about your friend or relative's life or thoughts.
- ☐ Include a friendly closing before your signature.

Revise a Friendly Letter

1. Use the checklist to evaluate this part of a draft for a friendly letter. What changes are needed?

_____

_____

_____

_____

_____

Revising Checklist

☐ Is your letter formatted correctly?

☐ Do any of the parts need more detail or explanation?

☐ Do you need to rearrange any details in a more effective order?

2. Revise this draft. Use revising marks to show your changes.

Revising

MARK	WHAT IT MEANS
∧	Insert something.
↶	Move to here.
∧—	Replace with this.
⸋	Take out.
¶	Make a new paragraph.

Dear Taeko,

When I visited the wildlife center, I learned about the center's work to help endangered species. First, my guide explained why the center works to help endangered animals. Then, I saw several animals in their natural habitats. I saw a huge turtle and a hummingbird. Before I walked home, I told my guide I'd love to volunteer at the center. Volunteers were feeding the animals and keeping track of the animals' health.

My guide said I could bring a friend to volunteer with me, so let me know if you're interested. We'd have a great time!

Your friend,

Tasha

3. Now use the checklist to help you revise the draft of your friendly letter on page 137.

© National Geographic Learning, a part of Cengage Learning, Inc.

Edit and Proofread

Grammar Workout: Check Adverbs

Add an adverb to modify the underlined word in each sentence.

1. I _____ <u>attached</u> my snorkel and fins.

2. Then I <u>dove</u> _____ beneath the water.

3. Snorkeling allowed me to see the fish _____ <u>closely</u>.

4. The _____ <u>brightly</u> colored fish were amazing.

5. My eyes <u>moved</u> _____ from one fish to another.

6. They all swam _____ <u>gracefully</u> in and around the rocky reef!

7. It was _____ <u>impossible</u> for me to stop watching.

8. But I _____ <u>returned</u> to the surface, thinking about when I could go again.

Spelling Workout: Check Adverbs Ending in *-ly*

Add *-ly* to change each adjective into an adverb.

1. happy _____

2. cool _____

3. able _____

4. steady _____

5. final _____

6. unbelievable _____

7. responsible _____

8. heavy _____

9. hopeful _____

10. noisy _____

Mechanics Workout: Check Apostrophes in Contractions

Find and fix any errors with apostrophes in contractions.

1. We should'nt ignore the giant panda's dwindling habitat.

2. Deforestation and overpopulation ar'ent the only problems.

3. Poachers still hunt the animals for their fur. This cant be tolerated!

4. This is why Im' asking others to support the conservation organizations' efforts to stop poaching.

5. Theyr'e the giant panda's best bet for survival.

Check Grammar, Spelling, and Mechanics

Proofread the letter. Check the spelling of adverbs with *-ly* and use of apostrophes. Add adverbs for interest. Correct the mistakes.

Editing and Proofreading Marks	
∧	Insert something.
∧	Add a comma.
∧	Add a semicolon.
⊙	Add a period.
⊙	Add a colon.
ѱ ѱ	Add quotation marks.
∨	Add apostrophe.
≡	Capitalize.
/	Make lower case.
ℒ	Delete.
¶	Make new paragraph.
◯	Check spelling.
⌒	Replace with this.
∿	Change order.
#	Insert space.
◡	Close up.

September 23, 2014

Hi Keisha,

Thanks for your letter. Im realy glad you like your new school.

Did I tell you I joined the student council? Were working hard on a lot of projects. The biggest one is a dance to raise money for the Endangered Species Fund. I was incrediblely pleased when my parents said the'yd help us out.

That's great that you arranged to come for a visit. It has been too long!

See you soon,

Jane

© National Geographic Learning, a part of Cengage Learning, Inc.

Edit and Proofread, continued

Edit and Proofread Your Friendly Letter

Now edit and proofread your work.

1. Use a checklist as you edit and proofread. Add things you are working on to the checklist.

2. Look to see which errors are marked most often. Jot down your top three trouble-spots.

_____

_____

_____

Remember to Check

- ☐ adverbs
- ☐ adverbs ending in *-ly*
- ☐ apostrophes in contractions
- ☐ _____
- ☐ _____

3. Ask your teacher about ways to fix these mistakes, or check out the Grammar Handbook for information.

Focus on Spelling

Improve your spelling by following these steps.

1. Create a personal spelling list. Record words that you misspelled. Look up correct spelling in the dictionary and add these words to **My Spelling List**.

2. Pick twelve words. Write each word four times. First write it in all lowercase letters. Next write it in all capital letters. After that, write the vowels in lowercase and the consonants in capital letters. Last, write the word using fancy letters that you create on your own. For example, your letters can be curly or tall and skinny.

3. Work with a partner to play **I'm Thinking of a Spelling Word**. Take turns giving each other clues. Some clues might be *I'm thinking of a word that rhymes with . . .* or *I'm thinking of a word that means . . .* With each clue, the answer should include the word and its spelling.

4. With a partner, play a scrambled-letter game. Take each other's spelling words and write them in scrambled form. See who can unscramble all the words first.

5. Use an audio recorder and record your words and their spelling. Then listen to your recording, checking to see that you spelled each word correctly.

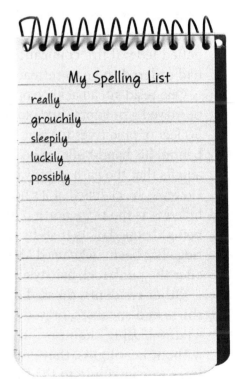

My Spelling List
really
grouchily
sleepily
luckily
possibly

Analyze a Story Scene

**What makes this story scene a good model?
Read the story scene and answer the questions.**

Clay Springs Renegades Defy Federal Mandate

by Alana Suarez

Clay Springs is a dirt-street town on a high plateau in Arizona. It has only one general store, a post office the size of a tool shed, and a volunteer fire department. With a population of about 150 people, this tiny town hardly seemed like a hotbed of rebellion.

But, with their homes at risk, every resident of Clay Springs who could operate a bulldozer, backhoe, chainsaw, or hose was called into action. These homeowners stubbornly defied federal fire commanders who had ordered them to retreat.

One resident, a backhoe operator, borrowed a bulldozer and plowed down 50 feet of pine trees to create a firebreak behind his hand-built log house. He admits that the gash in his yard is ugly. However, he claims that it's not nearly as hideous as the ridge north of town. Since being stripped of its trees by the fire, the ridge has been nicknamed Mohawk Hill after the punk-rock hairstyle.

Other residents, dressed only in tee-shirts and sneakers, braved the massive wildfire. Using chainsaws in the dark without headlights, they cut down trees to contribute to the firebreak.

Many officials have criticized the Clay Springs renegades for endangering themselves as well as the whole fire management system. Others applaud the wildcat efforts of the courageous residents. In the end, they saved all but three of their homes. And nobody was injured.

1. How does the writer get your attention right away?

_____

_____

_____

_____

_____

2. What are some vivid words and sensory details the writer uses?

_____

_____

_____

_____

_____

_____

3. What do you learn about the story scene from the writing? How does the writer show this?

_____

_____

_____

_____

_____

_____

_____

_____

© National Geographic Learning, a part of Cengage Learning, Inc.

Plan a Story Scene

Use pages 143–144 to plan your story scene.

1. What will you write about? List several subjects. Then choose the subject you think is the most interesting.

Ideas	Good and Bad Points

2. Complete your writing road map. Use the FATP chart. Be sure to identify your audience and purpose.

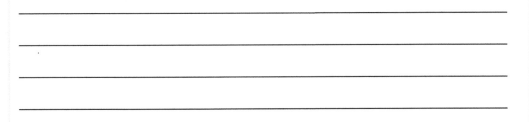

FATP Chart

Form: _story scene_

Audience: _____

Topic: _____

_____

Purpose: _____

_____

_____

_____

© National Geographic Learning, a part of Cengage Learning, Inc.

Level C
Project 11: Write to Describe

Writing Application: Prewrite

3. Use the web to gather details about your story scene.

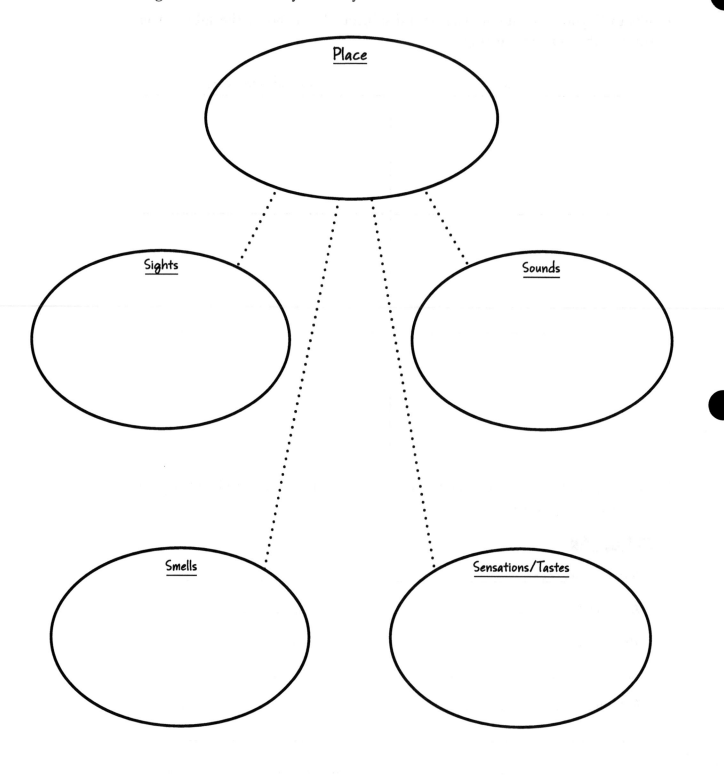

Draft a Story Scene

Use your plan from pages 143–144 to write the first draft of
your story scene.

Drafting Checklist

☐ Grab readers'
attention with
an interesting
introduction.

☐ Use vivid,
precise words
and sensory
details to give a
clear picture of
the story scene.

☐ Show where and
when the story
takes place.

_____

_____

_____

_____

_____

_____

_____

_____

_____

_____

_____

_____

_____

_____

_____

_____

_____

_____

_____

_____

_____

_____

_____

_____

_____

_____

_____

_____

Revise a Story Scene

1. Use the checklist to evaluate this draft of a story scene. What changes are needed?

_____

_____

_____

_____

_____

2. Revise the draft. Use revising marks to show your changes.

Revising

MARK	WHAT IT MEANS
∧	Insert something.
↶	Move to here.
⌃—	Replace with this.
⟋	Take out.
¶	Make a new paragraph.

Wildland Firefighter

Troy Matthews had wanted to be a firefighter all his life. But nothing had prepared him for the disorder that he faced tonight. Most fires are fairly predictable, but not wildland fires. That's what makes them so interesting. Tonight Troy was going to test his skills. The wind was blowing sagebrush stumps all over. Troy could almost taste the ashes in his mouth. Some big flames started to twirl around until they formed a giant funnel of fire. When Troy saw flames starting to lick at his truck, he jumped onto the hood and put out the flames. At last, the fire was under control. Tired but happy, Troy packed up his gear.

3. Now use the checklist to help you revise the draft of your story scene on page 145.

© National Geographic Learning, a part of Cengage Learning, Inc.

Edit and Proofread

Grammar Workout: Check for Complete Sentences

Turn the fragments into complete sentences.

1. The pony. It neighed as Anita led it out of the barn.

_____

2. Anita thought. The pony was ready to ride.

_____

3. Anita grabbed the pony's reins. Because of its rowdiness.

_____

4. Anita hopped onto the pony. Rode around the ring.

_____

5. Put her head back. She looked into the sky.

_____

Spelling Workout: Check Sound-Alike Words

Choose the correct sound-alike word from the parentheses to complete each sentence.

1. Anita walked the pony _____ the slippery area.
(passed, past)

2. To calm the pony, Anita gently stroked its _____ , brown mane.
(course, coarse)

3. Anita rode for over _____ hours.
(too, two)

4. Finally, she moved the reins to the _____ to head back to the stable.
(right, write)

5. Anita and the pony were ready _____ a rest.
(for, four)

© National Geographic Learning, a part of Cengage Learning, Inc.

Mechanics Workout: Check Commas in Lists

Use proofreading marks to fix the punctuation mistakes in the sentences.

1. Anita and the pony cantered past the barn the fields and the woods.

2. When the pony tried to jump over the river, he fell and injured his ankle leg and hoof.

3. Anita's dad, the vet and the trainer came to help.

4. That night, Anita covered the pony with a red white and blue blanket.

5. Anita her mom and her best friend Katie took turns checking up on the pony.

Check Grammar, Spelling, and Mechanics

Proofread the passage. Check the spelling for sound-alike words, for complete sentences, and for commas in lists. Correct the mistakes.

Editing and Proofreading Marks	
∧	Insert something.
⋏	Add a comma.
⋏	Add a semicolon.
⊙	Add a period.
⊙	Add a colon.
ⱽ ⱽ	Add quotation marks.
ⱽ	Add apostrophe.
≡	Capitalize.
/	Make lower case.
℘	Delete.
¶	Make new paragraph.
◯	Check spelling.
⌒	Replace with this.
∽	Change order.
#	Insert space.
◡	Close up.

Anita bundled up in her blew sweatshirt riding pants and boots. She couldn't wait to get out and visit her pony. She hoped the injury would not affect the pony's running jumping or happiness. Anita walked out to the barn. She didn't no what to expect. To her surprise. The pony was standing up in the stall. He neighed loudly. When he saw her coming. Anita was overjoyed excited and ecstatic. She reached up and began to stroke the pony's long main. The pony was not completely back to normal. But he was healing nicely.

Edit and Proofread, continued

Edit and Proofread Your Story Scene
Now edit and proofread your work.

1. Use a checklist as you edit and proofread. Add things you are working on to the checklist.

2. Look to see which errors are marked most often. Jot down your top three trouble spots.

_____

_____

_____

3. Ask your teacher about ways to fix these mistakes, or check out the Grammar Handbook for information.

Focus on Spelling
Improve your spelling by following these steps.

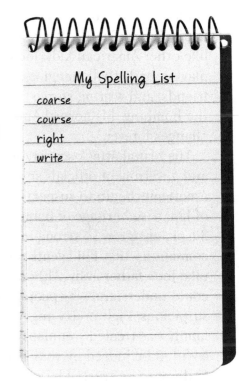

My Spelling List

coarse

course

right

write

1. Create a personal spelling list. Record words that you misspelled. Look up correct spelling in the dictionary and add these words to **My Spelling List**.

2. Pick twelve words. Make a colorful display of the words. Get a sheet of chart paper. Write each word three times in a different color.

3. Work with a partner to play **Spelling Tic-Tac-Toe**. Draw a tic-tac-toe board. Take turns asking each other to spell words. When a player spells a word correctly, that player gets to mark an X or an O on the game board. The game continues until one player is able to draw a vertical, diagonal, or horizontal line through the X's or O's.

4. Write the letters for each word on separate squares of paper. Attach the letters for each word to each other with a paper clip. Unscramble the letters to spell each of your words.

5. Invent your own memory strategy for difficult words. Think of a good way to remember *why* letters appear (or not) in a word.

Word	Explanation
dessert	"It has two s's for **s**weet **s**tuff!"

Analyze a Literary Analysis

What makes this literary analysis a good model?
Read the literary analysis and answer the questions.

Feature Checklist

A good literary analysis

☐ quickly summarizes what you've read

☐ expresses your personal thoughts and opinions about the literature

☐ supports your opinions with reasons and evidence from the text

☐ may mention a life lesson or important truth you learned from reading the text.

Thin Wood Walls

by David Patneaude

Reviewed by Maggie Fitzpatrick

I love reading about history but don't usually get too involved or emotional about the events. But when I read *Thin Wood Walls*, I couldn't put it down. I was mesmerized by what happened to a Japanese American family following the attack on Pearl Harbor in Hawaii on December 7, 1941.

Eleven-year-old Joe Hanada and his family live in Seattle, Washington. Just like other American kids, Joe enjoys playing basketball, hanging out with friends, and writing stories. But after the bombing, his normal American life changes forever.

The brutal attack scares Americans and government officials so much that Americans begin to suspect anyone of Japanese heritage of being a spy. Suspicions grow so strong in Joe's community that FBI agents unjustly take Joe's father away. Although I could understand why people were suspicious, I felt pretty angry that Joe's family was treated so unfairly. It'd feel awful to be judged by your heritage and not to be trusted by people in your own community!

1. **What does the reviewer say *Thin Wood Walls* is mostly about?**

   _____

   _____

   _____

   _____

   _____

2. **What is the writer's overall opinion about the book?**

   _____

   _____

   _____

   _____

   _____

3. **What details or evidence from the book does the writer include to support the idea that Joe's life changes forever?**

   _____

   _____

   _____

   _____

   _____

Analyze a Literary Analysis, continued

Then, the government orders all Japanese Americans living on the West Coast to move to internment camps. Sadly, Joe and his family have to leave their home. While he is living in a cell-like room with his entire family, Joe finds comfort in writing. He uses the journal his father gave him to write passages and haikus about his experiences. Joe gives a powerful description of the people he encounters, both good and bad, and the experience of feeling like the enemy.

Although the story is told from Joe's point of view, Joe is able to present many different viewpoints from other Japanese Americans. Some are eager to prove their loyalty to the United States, while others reject all things American. This gives the book an interesting take on a very controversial period in American history.

Since the book is written from Joe's point of view, I think it is really powerful. His detailed descriptions made me understand what he and his family experienced. The book showed me that life can be cruel and unfair, but you have to overcome it. Joe's ability to survive this experience and look at the situation from many angles is remarkable. I only hope I can face any hardships I might encounter in my future the way he did.

4. **What evidence does the writer use to support her opinion that the book gives an interesting take on this controversial period in American history?**

_____

_____

_____

_____

_____

5. **What is good about the writer's conclusion?**

_____

_____

_____

_____

_____

6. **What life lesson has the writer learned from reading the book?**

_____

_____

_____

_____

_____

Evaluate for Development of Ideas

Read each literary analysis. Use the rubric on page 153 to score each analysis for development of ideas. Explain your scores.

Writing Sample 1

Journey to America
by Sonia Levitin

This moving story tells of one Jewish family's difficult and dangerous escape from Nazi Germany. It shows how love and family can help people survive any obstacle.

The Holocaust had not yet started in 1938. Few people realized how dangerous the Nazis were. Lisa Platt's father did, so he escaped to America. He sent Lisa, her mother, and her sisters to safety in Switzerland until they could join him.

In Switzerland and America, the family faces poverty, separations, and starting over. When their mother becomes ill, for example, the three sisters must live with separate Swiss host families until she recovers. But they never lose touch with one another, and the dream of a reunion in America keeps them strong.

Score	1	2	3	4

_____
_____
_____
_____
_____
_____
_____
_____
_____

Writing Sample 2

Journey to America
by Sonia Levitin

This story was good. The Platt family leaves Germany and goes to America, but they don't all go together. The father goes first and the mother and sisters go later. They go to Switzerland before America.

I think the Nazis were cruel, but the family is very brave to move to another country. I don't know if I could leave my home and go to live somewhere else.

Score	1	2	3	4

_____
_____
_____
_____
_____
_____
_____
_____
_____
_____
_____

Evaluate for Development of Ideas, continued

Writing Rubric

Development of Ideas

	How thoughtful and interesting is the writing?	How well are the ideas or claims explained and supported?
4 Wow!	The writing engages the reader with meaningful ideas or claims and presents them in a way that is interesting and appropriate to the audience, purpose, and type of writing.	The ideas or claims are fully explained and supported. • The ideas or claims are well developed with important details, evidence, and/or description. • The writing feels complete, and the reader is satisfied.
3 Ahh.	<u>Most</u> of the writing engages the reader with meaningful ideas or claims and presents them in a way that is interesting and appropriate to the audience, purpose, and type of writing.	<u>Most</u> of the ideas or claims are explained and supported. • Most of the ideas or claims are developed with important details, evidence, and/or description. • The writing feels mostly complete, but the reader still has some questions.
2 Hmm.	<u>Some</u> of the writing engages the reader with meaningful ideas or claims and presents them in a way that is interesting and appropriate to the audience, purpose, and type of writing.	<u>Some</u> of the ideas or claims are explained and supported. • Only some of the ideas or claims are developed. Details, evidence, and/or description are limited or not relevant. • The writing leaves the reader with many questions.
1 Huh?	The writing does <u>not</u> engage the reader. It is not appropriate to the audience, purpose, and type of writing.	The ideas or claims are <u>not</u> explained or supported. The ideas or claims lack details, evidence, and/or description, and the writing leaves the reader unsatisfied.

Raise the Score

1. Use the rubric on page 153 to evaluate and score this literary analysis.

Score	1	2	3	4

Nadia the Willful
by Sue Alexander

"Nadia the Willful" is a story about a girl who found a way to ease her wicked temper and was praised throughout the land. The Bedouin people began to call her Nadia the Wise instead. It is a fascinating story.

In the story, Nadia's brother Hamed is the only person who can calm Nadia's temper and make her laugh. Nadia feels lost when Hamed dies, and she becomes angry and depressed. She only feels better when she thinks and speaks of her brother. One day, when a young shepherd speaks of Hamed, Nadia's father bans the shepherd from the kingdom. Nadia and her father later make up and Nadia becomes admired by her people.

The first part of the story was very sad, like when Nadia and her father searched for Hamed. I felt bad because their search was not successful.

"Nadia the Willful" is good and inspiring because of the ending. I wonder what would have happened if Nadia had never spoken Hamed's name.

2. Explain what the writer should do to raise the score:

_____

_____

_____

_____

_____

_____

_____

_____

_____

© National Geographic Learning, a part of Cengage Learning, Inc.

Raise the Score, continued

3. **Now revise the literary analysis on page 154 to improve the development of ideas. Write your revised analysis here.**

_____
_____
_____
_____
_____
_____
_____
_____
_____
_____
_____
_____
_____
_____
_____
_____
_____
_____
_____
_____
_____
_____
_____
_____
_____
_____
_____
_____
_____
_____
_____

Write Good Beginnings and Endings

A. Read the paragraph. Write some new beginning sentences for the paragraph that will do a better job of grabbing the reader's interest.

> Maurine F. Dahlberg's book *Escape to West Berlin* is very interesting. *Escape to West Berlin* tells the story of a young girl named Heidi who lives in East Berlin, Germany. Heidi's dad lives in East Berlin but works in West Berlin. So, he is considered a "border crosser," or a traitor. As a result, Heidi and her family experience harsh treatment from the government, as well as from close friends. They decide to flee East Berlin. They hope to find safety and freedom in the West. This journey forces Heidi to be brave and face many fears.

1. Use a thought-provoking question or statistic.

_____

_____

_____

2. Start with a quotation.

_____

_____

_____

3. Begin with a personal connection.

_____

_____

_____

© National Geographic Learning, a part of Cengage Learning, Inc.

Write Good Beginnings and Endings, continued

B. Read the paragraphs from a literary analysis. Write a good ending that summarizes the writer's ideas.

Steps to Summarize

☐ Read the paper carefully.
☐ Restate the main ideas.
☐ Condense important details.

Escape to West Berlin
by Maurine F. Dahlberg

What if your town was divided in half? What if the half that you lived in didn't allow you to be free? Would you risk your life to cross to the other side? Heidi Klenk and her family take that risk in *Escape to West Berlin*. This book taught me about an important part of world history that I didn't know much about. It also caught my interest because it featured a brave main character and had an exciting plot.

When the East German government closes the border to the West, people living in East Berlin are forced to stay in East Germany and live under communist rule. Heidi's family members are considered traitors because they are "border crossers" and want to live in the West. As the Klenks start to fear for their safety, they decide to cross over to West Berlin illegally. In the process, Heidi gets separated from her family. She must face her fears and find the courage to take the dangerous journey on her own.

Reading this story made me feel like I was there with Heidi. Before reading this book, I didn't know much about the division of Germany. Now, I feel like I've experienced the life of an East German girl through Heidi's eyes.

_____

_____

_____

_____

_____

C. Write some more good endings for the paragraphs on a separate sheet of paper. End with a question, personal example, or quotation; or revisit the main point.

Explain and Support Your Ideas

Read the following paragraph from a literary analysis of "Passage to Freedom."
Improve the paragraph by adding specific reasons and evidence to explain and support the ideas.

"Passage to Freedom: The Sugihara Story," by Ken Mochizuki, is a story about how a young boy's life changed forever. He watched his father help many Jewish refugees find safety. The boy was impressed by his father's selfless behavior and determination. It is an inspiring story that shows how far some people are willing to go in order to help those in need.

1. Write down facts and evidence from the story that could be included in this paragraph.

_____

_____

_____

_____

2. Write down examples from the story that support the paragraph's ideas.

_____

_____

_____

_____

_____

3. Write down direct quotations from the story that support the ideas and examples.

_____

_____

_____

_____

_____

Explain and Support Your Ideas, continued

4. Write down your own thoughts about the story.

_____

_____

_____

_____

_____

5. Use the facts, details, examples, quotations, and thoughts you gathered in steps 1–4 to write a new version of the paragraph. Make sure to explain and support your ideas with evidence from the story.

_____

_____

_____

_____

_____

_____

_____

_____

_____

_____

_____

_____

_____

_____

_____

_____

_____

_____

_____

Plan a Literary Analysis

Use pages 160–161 to plan your literary analysis.

1. Choose a book that means a lot to you. List three or four books you feel strongly about. Circle the book you choose.

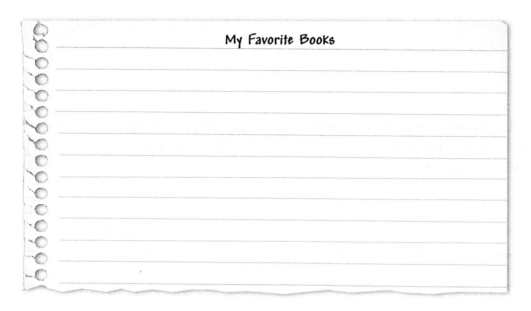

My Favorite Books

2. Once you have reread or reviewed your book, record your thoughts in the chart below. Summarize all your important ideas.

Book

Thoughts and reactions

What's good about it?

Would I recommend this to others? Why or why not?

Plan a Literary Analysis, continued

3. Gather support for your opinions. Use an opinion chart to help you get organized.

Opinion

Supporting reasons and evidence

Opinion

Supporting reasons and evidence

Opinion

Supporting reasons and evidence

Draft a Literary Analysis

Use your plan from pages 160–161 to write the first draft of your
literary analysis.

Use your plan from pages 160–161 to write the first draft of your

Drafting Checklist

- ☐ Quickly summarize what you have read.
- ☐ Express your personal thoughts about the literature.
- ☐ Engage readers with worthwhile ideas.
- ☐ Support your opinions with reasons and evidence from the text.
- ☐ Mention a life lesson or important truth you learned from reading the text.

_____

_____

_____

_____

Draft a Literary Analysis, continued

Revise a Literary Analysis

1. Use the checklist to evaluate this draft of a literary analysis. What changes are needed?

_____

_____

_____

_____

_____

2. Revise the draft. Use revising marks to show your changes.

Revising

MARK	WHAT IT MEANS
∧	Insert something.
⌒	Move to here.
⌜	Replace with this.
⚊℣	Take out.
¶	Make a new paragraph.

Farewell to Manzanar

Farewell to Manzanar tells the true story of a young Japanese American girl named Jeanne. I learned a lot about a forgotten point in American history.

During World War II, America was at war with Germany and Japan. The government forced thousands of Japanese Americans into camps. Jeanne and her family were sent to a camp called Manzanar. The upsetting experience of being taken away from their home changed them forever.

Jeanne also discusses her own identity issues. Before and after camp life, she had difficulty fitting in. She also clashed with her father.

3. Now use the checklist to help you revise the draft of your literary analysis on pages 162–163.

© National Geographic Learning, a part of Cengage Learning, Inc.

Edit and Proofread

Grammar Workout: Check Compound and Complex Sentences

CONJUNCTIONS		
and	although	or
but	because	since

Combine each pair of sentences. Tell if you formed a compound or complex sentence.

1. *The Freedom Writers Diary* is a great book. It inspires students to express their feelings.

_____

_____

2. I don't like to write essays for class. I love to write in my journal.

_____

_____

3. This book shows that all types of writing are important. You should always write with your heart.

_____

_____

4. I would love to have my journal published. I would have to remove some embarrassing entries.

_____

_____

Spelling Workout: Check Words You Have to Know or Look Up

Find and fix the spelling mistake in each sentence.

1. The reasen I relate to the teacher in the book is because she is a lot like my social studies teacher.

2. Every morning, Mr. Davis asks us to write down our thoughts on currant events.

3. It is interesting to see how our concurns change as we get more information on an issue.

4. Just like in the book, our teacher happons to want us to discover why we have certain opinions.

Mechanics Workout: Check Punctuation in Longer Sentences

Correctly punctuate the sentences. Add a comma or semicolon where it belongs.

1. Reading about Miep Gies was amazing she's an inspirational woman.

2. Her accounts of Anne Frank were very fascinating and they affected me on a personal level.

3. It was interesting to see that Ms. Gruwell's students had similar reactions even though I'm very different from them.

4. I would love to have Miep Gies visit my class it would be such an honor.

Check Grammar, Spelling, and Mechanics

Proofread the passage. Check the spelling of words you have to know, compound and complex sentences, and the punctuation in longer sentences. Correct the mistakes.

Editing and Proofreading Marks	
∧	Insert something.
⋏	Add a comma.
⋏	Add a semicolon.
⊙	Add a period.
⊙	Add a colon.
᯼ ᯼	Add quotation marks.
᯾	Add apostrophe.
≡	Capitalize.
╱	Make lower case.
℘	Delete.
¶	Make new paragraph.
◯	Check spelling.
⌒	Replace with this.
∽	Change order.
#	Insert space.
◡	Close up.

Reading a book about young writers was incredibel. I really enjoyed learning about their thoughts and opinions and how they are similar to my own. Some students felt exactly the same way I do some felt completly different. One student in particulur did not feel that Miep Gies was a hero I couldn't disagree more. I think all young people should read this book they can learn how to express their feelings. This book deminstrates that students can either let their emotions out on paper or they can let them out with terribel behavior.

© National Geographic Learning, a part of Cengage Learning, Inc.

Edit and Proofread, continued

Edit and Proofread Your Literary Analysis

Now edit and proofread your work.

1. Use a checklist as you edit and proofread. Add things you are working on to the checklist.

2. Look to see which errors are marked most often. Jot down your top three trouble spots.

_____

_____

_____

3. Ask your teacher about ways to fix these mistakes, or check out the Grammar Handbook for information.

Focus on Spelling

Improve your spelling by following these steps.

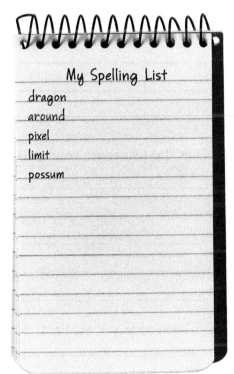

My Spelling List
dragon
around
pixel
limit
possum

1. Create a personal spelling list. Record words that you misspelled. Look up correct spelling in the dictionary and add these words to **My Spelling List**.

2. Pick twelve words. Make each word look interesting and special by tracing it five times. Write the word in one color. Then trace it four more times in four different colors. Say each letter to yourself as you trace it.

3. Work with a partner to play **Spelling Catch**. Pitch words to each other by saying "Here's the windup. Here's the pitch. The word is . . ." Take turns pitching. The first "batter" to spell ten words correctly wins.

4. Write each spelling word three times. The first time, just write the word. The second time, write it and then circle all the consonants. The third time, write it and circle all the vowels.

5. Play **Memory** to help you remember your words. Write each spelling word on two different index cards. Mix up the cards and place them face down. Turn the cards over two at a time. Your goal is to find the matching cards. Say and spell the words on the cards you turn over. If you make a match, remove those cards from the game. You've won when you've removed all the cards.

Publish, Share, and Reflect

Publish and Share Your Literary Analysis

Check the final formats you used to publish your literary analysis. Then answer the following questions.

Publishing

What was the final format of your project?	How did you share your project?
☐ Wrote it neatly by hand	☐ Shared it with a large group
☐ Typed it on a computer	☐ Shared it with a small group

1. Whether you published it by hand or on the computer, what did you do to dress up your final project?

_____

_____

_____

_____

_____

2. How did you share your work? What did you learn through sharing your work?

_____

_____

_____

_____

_____

_____

_____

_____

_____

_____

_____

_____

_____

Publish, Share, and Reflect, continued

Reflect on Your Literary Analysis
Read your literary analysis. Then answer questions 1–6.

1. What do you like best about your work? _____

_____

_____

2. What did you do well? _____

_____

_____

3. What could you improve about your work? _____

_____

_____

_____

4. Did you learn more about why this book means a lot to you? _____

_____

_____

5. Did you express your feelings well in your analysis? Did you provide reasons and evidence for your opinions? _____

_____

_____

6. Will you add your literary analysis to your Writing Portfolio? Explain your decision.

❑ Yes, I will add this to my Writing Portfolio.

_____

_____

❑ No, I will not add this to my Writing Portfolio.

_____

_____

Build a Cause-and-Effect Paragraph

1. The events below are out of order. Write each event in the cause-and-effect chain in an order that makes sense.

- He thought he could use his knowledge in a different way.

- His team played well together and won the league championship.

- My older brother Theo didn't make the high school basketball team.

- He was upset because he loves basketball and knows a lot about it.

- After the end of the season, Theo realized he enjoyed coaching more than playing.

- Theo decided to volunteer as a coach for a youth basketball team.

Cause-and-Effect Chain

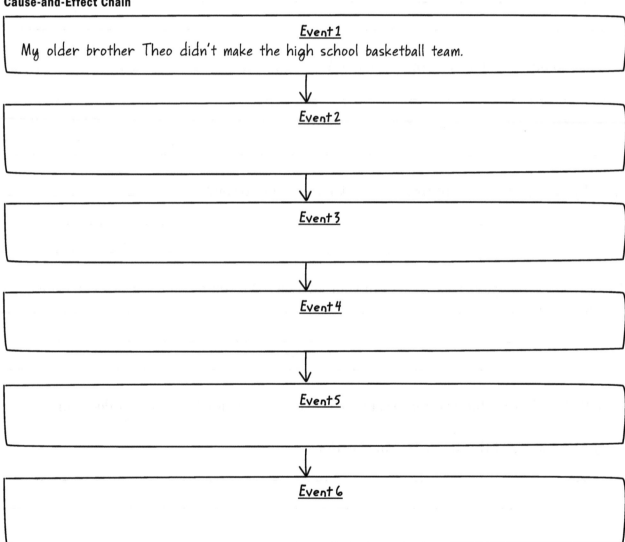

Event 1
My older brother Theo didn't make the high school basketball team.

Event 2

Event 3

Event 4

Event 5

Event 6

2. Now that your causes and effects are in order, write out the chain of events in paragraph form on a separate sheet of paper.

Plan a Cause-and-Effect Paragraph

Use pages 171–172 to plan your cause-and-effect paragraph.

1. Quickly brainstorm topic, audience, and form ideas for your cause-and-effect paragraph.

Topic	Audience	Form

2. Use this cause-and-effect chain to organize your thoughts.

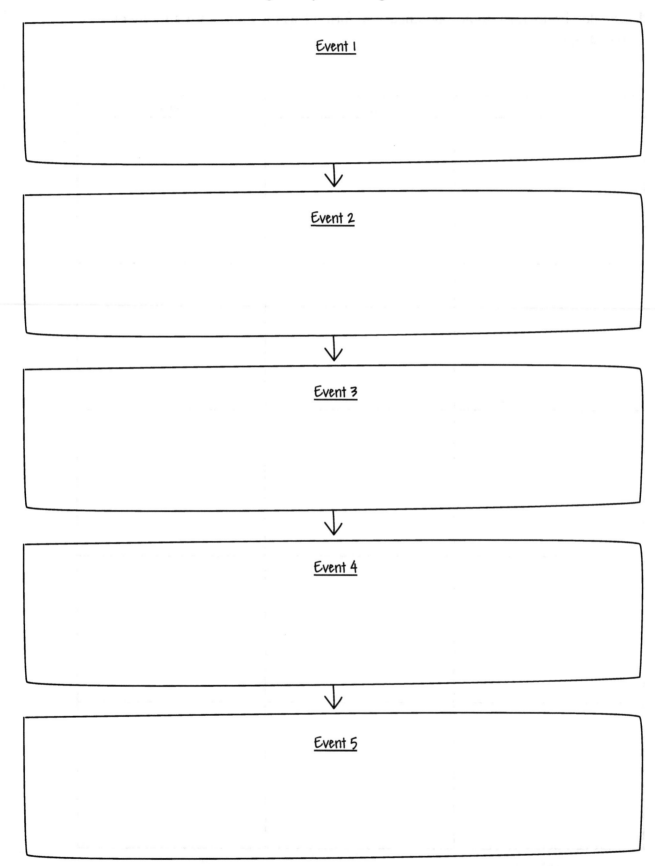

Event 1

Event 2

Event 3

Event 4

Event 5

Draft a Cause-and-Effect Paragraph

Use your plan from pages 171–172 to write the first draft of your cause-and-effect paragraph.

Drafting Checklist

- ☐ Start with a good topic sentence.
- ☐ Present causes and effects in logical order.
- ☐ Use signal words to show causes and effects.
- ☐ Show why the event was unfair and how it affected you.

_____

_____

_____

_____

_____

_____

_____

_____

_____

_____

_____

_____

_____

_____

_____

_____

_____

_____

_____

_____

_____

_____

Revise a Cause-and-Effect Paragraph

1. Use the checklist to evaluate this draft of a
   cause-and-effect paragraph. What changes
   are needed?

_____

_____

_____

_____

_____

2. Revise this draft. Use revising marks to show your changes.

Revising

MARK	WHAT IT MEANS
∧	Insert something.
↶	Move to here.
∧—	Replace with this.
˘	Take out.
⁋	Make a new paragraph.

Views

Ms. Lang had her class sit in alphabetical order. Becky

Roland had to sit behind Al Rodriguez because Roland comes

after Rodriguez. Becky was the shortest of all the students in

the class. Al was the tallest of all the students in the class.

Becky had to sit on her knees and peer over Al's head. Al felt

bad for blocking Becky's view, so he slouched down in his seat.

Ms. Lang noticed the students' discomfort. Becky had bruises

on her knees and Al had a crick in his neck. Ms. Lang decided

that it would be fairer to arrange the students' seats according

to height.

3. Now use the checklist to help you revise the draft of your cause-and-effect
   paragraph on page 173.

Edit and Proofread

Grammar Workout: Check Participles as Adjectives

Turn the verb into a present participle or past participle. Use the participle as an adjective to complete the sentence.

1. Terry didn't tell Mrs. Thompson about our _____ research.
(miss)

2. _____, he had waited until the last minute.
(delay)

3. Then a _____ message, *Call Tech Support Help*, appeared on his
computer. (flash)

4. _____, I started reading.
(tremble)

5. _____, Mrs. Thompson tapped her pen on the desk.
(disturb)

6. My _____ classmates tried to hide their laughter.
(amuse)

Spelling Workout: Check Sound-Alike Words

Complete each sentence with the correct spelling.

1. Mrs. Thompson said, "I am disappointed in you _____."
(to, two)

2. "What happened to _____ report?" she asked.
(your, you're)

3. "_____ were problems with my computer," started Terry. "It was broken,
(Their, There)
so I couldn't do all the research."

4. Mrs. Thompson sighed. "_____ not telling the whole truth, Terry,"
(Your, You're)
she said.

5. "Well, _____ just that . . . " Terry mumbled, embarrassed.
(its, it's)

Mechanics Workout: Check Apostrophes in Contractions

Write contractions for the words in parentheses.

1. Terry finally looked at Mrs. Thompson. "_____ right," he said. **(You are)**

2. "_____ not Miriam's fault," Terry continued. **(It is)**

3. "Wait, Terry!" I said. "_____ not fair! We were partners!" **(That is)**

4. "I _____ understand," said Mrs. Thompson. **(do not)**

5. "_____ you explain it better?" she asked. **(Can not)**

Check Grammar, Spelling, and Mechanics

Proofread the passage. Check the spelling and the use of participles as adjectives and apostrophes. Correct the mistakes.

Editing and Proofreading Marks	
∧	Insert something.
∧	Add a comma.
∧	Add a semicolon.
⊙	Add a period.
⊙	Add a colon.
ᵛ ᵛ	Add quotation marks.
ᵛ	Add apostrophe.
≡	Capitalize.
/	Make lower case.
℘	Delete.
¶	Make new paragraph.
◯	Check spelling.
⌐	Replace with this.
∼	Change order.
#	Insert space.
◡	Close up.

I couldnt believe I was in this situation. Mrs. Thompson stood right there looking at us, while Terry and I had our eyes focused on the polishing floor. "Cant you explain yourselves?" she said. Terry looked like he felt bad, two.

"Its my fault, Mrs. Thompson," Terry began. "I thought their would be more time, so I put off this project and didnt do anything." Terry looked up, and with his glistening, eyes said, "Please dont blame Miriam."

"Your finally telling me the truth," said Mrs. Thompson. "You shouldn't have put off your assigning project until the last minute, but Im willing to give you another chance. I want the report on my desk tomorrow, and dont let it happen again."

Edit and Proofread, continued

Edit and Proofread Your Paragraph

Now edit and proofread your work.

1. Use a checklist as you edit and proofread.
Add things you are working on to the checklist.

2. Look to see which errors are marked most often.
Jot down your top three trouble spots.

_____

_____

_____

3. Ask your teacher about ways to fix these mistakes, or check out the
Grammar Handbook for information.

Remember to Check

- ☐ participles as adjectives
- ☐ spelling of sound-alike words
- ☐ apostrophes in contractions
- ☐ _____
- ☐ _____

Focus on Spelling

Improve your spelling by following these steps.

1. Create a personal spelling list. Record words that you
misspelled. Look up correct spelling in the dictionary and
add these words to **My Spelling List**.

2. Pick twelve words. Focus on four words each day. Write
your words before each meal and check the spelling. At
the end of the week, try writing all twelve words.

3. Work with a partner to play **Spelling Behind Your Back**.
Have a partner stand with his or her back to the board.
List your partner's spelling words on the board. Say each
word and ask your partner to spell it. Switch roles.

4. Organize your words into lists. List them from shortest to
longest word. Next list them from easiest to hardest. Then
list them in reverse alphabetical order.

5. Invent your own acronyms to memorize difficult words. Think of a word that
begins with each letter. The words in the correct order should be easy for you
to remember. For example:

Spelling Word	Acronym
ocean	**o**ctopus, **c**oral, **e**el, **a**re **n**ear

My Spelling List

two
there
too
you're
their

Analyze a Cause-and-Effect Essay

What makes this cause-and-effect essay a good model?
Read the essay and answer the questions.

Creating a Central Government

by Kiri Liu

One of the main goals of the writers of the U.S. Constitution was to create a way to avoid tyranny, or the abuse of power, in the state and national governments. As a result, our founding fathers created a system of checks and balances, which prevents one branch of government from exercising too much power.

Before creating the Constitution, leaders in the United States drafted a document called the Articles of Confederation. The leaders feared an overpowering central government. So, they ultimately gave the majority of power to state governments. Each state government operated independently and had no strong national government to answer to. But this also meant that there was no way to prevent states from abusing their power. There was also no way to force state governments to cooperate with one another. As a result, state officials realized that it was nearly impossible to operate a united nation without centralization. So, the nation's leaders gathered once again to draft a new plan for the government, in the form of the Constitution.

Creating a plan for a strong central government was tricky. Because many early Americans had experienced life under an oppressive government by England, they wanted to avoid creating a similar government in the United States.

Feature Checklist

A good cause-and-effect essay

☐ presents one or more causes that lead to one or more effects

☐ includes an introduction, body, and conclusion.

1. How does the writer introduce the subject?

_____

_____

_____

_____

_____

_____

_____

_____

_____

2. How can you tell that this is a cause-and-effect essay?

_____

_____

_____

_____

_____

_____

_____

_____

_____

_____

_____

_____

Analyze a Cause-and_Effect Essay, continued

By creating the checks-and-balances system, no one branch of government could act without another branch "checking" its power. The U.S. Constitution requires three branches of government—judicial, executive, and legislative. Each branch of government has specific powers that the other branches do not have.

The system of checks and balances can be illustrated by the law-making process. In the national government, Congress has the ability to pass a bill proposing a law. However, the president has the ability to veto that bill to keep it from becoming a law. Congress, in turn, can override the president's veto with a two-thirds vote of both the Senate and the House of Representatives. Even if Congress and the president pass a law, the Supreme Court has the power to declare that law unconstitutional. This is just one example of the system in action. There are many other ways in which the branches can check one another's power.

The checks-and-balances system is still going strong today. Rifts still occur sometimes among the three branches of government. However, the mistakes of the past have helped our national government operate without one branch abusing its power.

3. **How does the writer link the causes and effects? Give an example.**

_____

_____

_____

_____

_____

_____

_____

_____

4. **How does the writer organize the body paragraphs? Is the organization effective?**

_____

_____

_____

_____

_____

_____

5. **What is good about the conclusion?**

_____

_____

_____

_____

_____

_____

_____

Evaluate for Voice and Style

Read each essay. Use the rubric on page 181 to score each essay for voice and style. Explain your scores.

Writing Sample 1

Education Reform

American schools have been falling behind other countries for years, especially in science and math. As a result, many parents are worried that public schools are failing their children.

In Philadelphia, the school system formed a partnership with a private company, Edison Schools, which creates charter schools. Thanks to their curriculum, test scores in Philadelphia schools have increased. Thousands of students have become proficient in math and science.

If these results are publicized, more partnerships like the one in Philadelphia will be started in other cities. When parents see results, they will want the same for their children.

Score	1	2	3	4

_____

_____

_____

_____

_____

_____

_____

_____

_____

Writing Sample 2

Digital Education

Educational reform is defined as a change in educational theory on a large scale. Educational reform is important. Technology is more widespread than ever before.

Right now, software called Digital Education is being developed. This software will change education entirely. This software will create classes for students to take online. No one would have to go to school. How great is that?

Digital Education would create classes for students using an academic profile. Math classes are hard to take in an online environment.

More changes like this should be made available to improve education in the 21st century.

Score	1	2	3	4

_____

_____

_____

_____

_____

_____

_____

_____

_____

Evaluate for Voice and Style, continued

Writing Rubric		

Voice and Style

	Does the writing have a clear voice, and is it the best style for the type of writing?	Is the language interesting and are the words and sentences appropriate for the purpose, audience, and type of writing?
4 Wow!	The writing <u>fully</u> engages the reader with its individual voice. The writing style is best for the type of writing.	The words and sentences are interesting and appropriate to the purpose and audience. · The words are precise and engaging. · The sentences are varied and flow together smoothly.
3 Ahh.	<u>Most</u> of the writing engages the reader with an individual voice. The writing style is mostly best for the type of writing.	<u>Most</u> of the words and sentences are interesting and appropriate to the purpose and audience. · Most words are precise and engaging. · Most sentences are varied and flow together.
2 Hmm.	<u>Some</u> of the writing engages the reader, but it has no individual voice and the style is not best for the writing type.	<u>Some</u> of the words and sentences are interesting and appropriate to the purpose and audience. · Some words are precise and engaging. · Some sentences are varied, but the flow could be smoother.
1 Huh?	The writing does <u>not</u> engage the reader.	<u>Few or none</u> of the words and sentences are appropriate to the purpose and audience. · The words are often vague and dull. · The sentences lack variety and do not flow together.

Raise the Score

1. Use the rubric on page 181 to evaluate and score this essay.

Score	1	2	3	4

A New System for a Fair Election

Are you concerned that your voice is not being heard? Do you think school elections are unfair? Well the election committee at Westfield Middle School gets your concerns. So, they are making sure that the opinions of the eighth-grade student body are really heard in this year's race for student council president. Last year, students said that the election was wrong. Many claimed that some students voted more than once. Just for the record, I only voted once! The school is going to change the way students vote.

This year, all students must register as a voter in order to be able to vote in the student council election. This will help the election committee keep track of every vote. The votes will be kept a secret, and voters will be given a number to use while voting instead of their name. This sounds way too confusing, but the election committee told me it should work.

As a result of this new system, the election committee can be sure that no students have voted more than once. The candidates are happy about this new system. The eighth-grade student body is as well. Because of this change, they know that this year's election will really show the voice of the voters.

2. Explain what the writer should do to raise the score:

_____

_____

_____

_____

_____

_____

_____

© National Geographic Learning, a part of Cengage Learning, Inc.

Raise the Score, continued

3. **Now revise the essay on page 182 to improve its voice and style. Write your revised essay here.**

_____
_____
_____
_____
_____
_____
_____
_____
_____
_____
_____
_____
_____
_____
_____
_____
_____
_____
_____
_____
_____
_____
_____
_____
_____
_____
_____

Choose the Right Voice

Study the FATP chart below. Then read the article at right and answer the questions.

FATP Chart

Form: _newspaper editorial_

Audience: _readers of a newspaper_

Topic: _Amber Alert_

Purpose: _to persuade_

1. Is the writer's tone appropriate for the audience? Explain your answer.

_____

_____

_____

_____

_____

_____

_____

2. Does the word choice seem appropriate for a persuasive piece? Explain your answer.

_____

_____

_____

_____

_____

_____

3. If you answered yes to Item 2, circle examples of appropriate voice in the text. If you answered no, use revising marks to show how you would change it.

Improve Your Alertness

The loss and abduction of children in our nation is a serious issue. It calls for our utmost attention. Our law enforcement agencies work extremely hard to successfully reunite missing children with their families. The AMBER Alert Program is a vital part of their success.

An AMBER Alert is used to notify people in a particular area that a child is missing. Once the child is reported, law officials notify broadcasters, transportation agencies, and wireless telephone companies. These groups then send out a message to the public asking them to keep watch for the child.

As a result of this program, 389 children have been returned to their families. In order to make this program more successful, every person needs to sign up to receive AMBER Alerts on his or her wireless phone. Since not everyone is always by a TV or a radio, this important information can be missed. This tiny effort can make a big difference to the family of a missing child. Go to the AMBER Alert Program Web site and sign up to receive these important wireless messages. Do it today! This small step could make you a hero.

Choose the Right Voice, continued

Study the FATP chart below. Then read the article at right and answer the questions.

FATP Chart

Form: _mazazine article_

Audience: _students and teachers_

Topic: _Suffragists/Silent Sentinel_

Purpose: _to inspire and motivate_

1. Is the writer's tone appropriate for the audience and purpose? Explain your answer.

_____

_____

_____

_____

_____

_____

_____

2. Does the word choice seem appropriate for a inspirational essay? Explain your answer.

_____

_____

_____

_____

_____

_____

_____

3. If you answered yes to Item 2, circle examples of appropriate voice in the text. If you answered no, use revising marks to show how you would change it.

The 19th Amendment

Women have only had the right to vote since the 19th Amendment to the Constitution was ratified in 1920. The road to getting the amendment ratified was not an easy one.

A group of many activists worked for years to call attention to the cause of women's suffrage, or voting rights. A group of women who called themselves the Silent Sentinels showed their support in a unique way. They protested by sitting in front of the White House for 18 months.

The 19th Amendment was originally proposed in 1918. That year the House of Representatives approved it. Then, the Senate defeated it by three votes.

As a result, the suffrage activists went into action. They campaigned for voters to get rid of senators who were opposed to women's suffrage. They accomplished what they wanted. The newly elected Senate approved the amendment. The process of ratification by the states finally got started.

The 19th Amendment was signed into law on August 26, 1920. Because of the efforts of the Silent Sentinels, all American citizens have the right to vote.

Use Figurative Language

**A. An idiom is a familiar expression that's not literally true.
Explain the meaning of each underlined idiom.**

1. I wish I could vote for both candidates, but <u>you can't have your cake
and eat it too</u>!

   _____

   _____

2. You can't <u>monkey around</u> with voting; you have to take it seriously.

   _____

   _____

3. A lot of people think that politics is <u>for the birds</u>, but they couldn't be
more wrong.

   _____

   _____

4. The candidates will <u>fight tooth and nail</u> until the election is over.

   _____

   _____

**B. A simile compares two unlike things using the words *like* or *as*.
Write your interpretation of each simile.**

1. The people at the political rally were like a crowd of fans waiting to greet
a celebrity. _____

   _____

2. Our government runs like a well-oiled machine. _____

   _____

3. Participating in a presidential race is as exhausting as running a marathon.

   _____

   _____

4. The Secret Service is like a team of worker bees. _____

   _____

Use Figurative Language, continued

C. A metaphor compares two unlike things by saying one thing *is* the other thing. Write your interpretation of each metaphor.

1. Congress is a symphony, and the Speaker its conductor.

_____

_____

2. The tunnels under the Capitol are a rat's maze of hallways and passages.

_____

_____

3. The Capitol Building is a sentinel over the city.

_____

_____

4. The Potomac River is a snake through the center of the city.

_____

_____

D. Write an example of an idiom, a simile, and a metaphor. Explain what each means.

Idiom: _____

Meaning: _____

_____

_____

Simile: _____

Meaning: _____

_____

_____

Metaphor: _____

Meaning: _____

_____

_____

Plan a Cause-and-Effect Essay

Use pages 188–189 to plan your cause-and-effect essay.

1. Choose a topic for your essay. Choose an issue that has clear causes and effects. Use a chart to brainstorm ideas. Then circle the topic you choose.

Ideas	Cause-and-effect questions	Possible causes or effects

2. Once you've decided on a topic, identify the most important thing you have to say in your essay. This is your central idea. Write it in one sentence.

_____

_____

_____

_____

_____

Plan a Cause-and-Effect Essay, continued

3. Use a cause-and-effect chart to organize your thoughts.

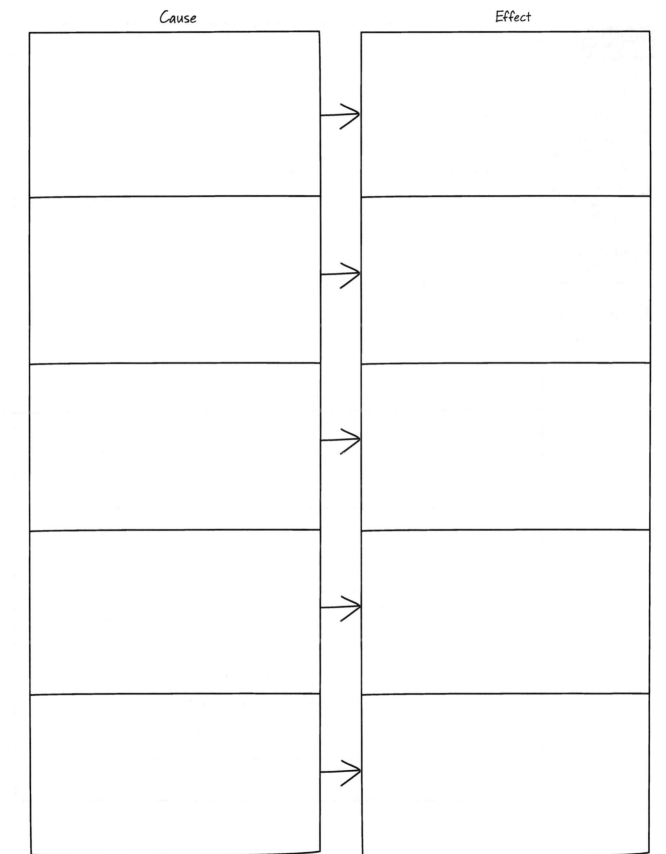

Cause   Effect

Draft a Cause-and-Effect Essay

Use your plan from pages 188–189 to write the first draft of your cause-and-effect essay.

© National Geographic Learning, a part of Cengage Learning, Inc.

Drafting Checklist

- ☐ Include an introduction, a body, and a conclusion.
- ☐ Focus on one cause and effect at a time.
- ☐ Use signal words to make causes and effects clear.
- ☐ Adapt your voice to your topic, form, audience, and purpose.
- ☐ Use vivid words and a variety of sentence types.

_____

_____

_____

_____

_____

_____

_____

_____

_____

_____

_____

_____

_____

_____

_____

_____

_____

_____

_____

_____

_____

_____

_____

_____

_____

Draft a Cause-and-Effect Essay, continued

_____

_____

_____

_____

_____

_____

_____

_____

_____

_____

_____

_____

_____

_____

_____

_____

_____

_____

_____

_____

_____

_____

_____

_____

_____

_____

_____

_____

_____

_____

_____

_____

Revise a Cause-and-Effect Essay

1. Use the checklist to evaluate this draft of a cause-and-effect essay. What changes are needed?

_____

_____

_____

_____

Revising Checklist

☐ Do you need to add more precise and specific details?

☐ Do you need to delete or consolidate any repeated ideas?

☐ Do you need to move any sentences to clarify the order of events?

☐ Do you need to add any transitions or signal words to improve flow?

2. Revise this draft. Use revising marks to show your changes.

Revising	
MARK	**WHAT IT MEANS**
∧	Insert something.
↻	Move to here.
⋏—	Replace with this.
⸓	Take out.
¶	Make a new paragraph.

Pond to Park

Ian Rice walked past the retention pond every day on his way to school. Ian had the idea to make a park around the pond. The pond was good for collecting rainwater, but he thought it could also be useful in other ways.

With the help of his parents, Ian drew up a plan to create the park. The plan included many details. Ian presented his plan to the city council. His presentation was impressive. The city council approved Ian's plan.

After a few months of construction, the park was completed in five months. City residents are enjoying the new open space.

3. Now use the checklist to help you revise the draft of your cause-and-effect essay on pages 190–191.

© National Geographic Learning, a part of Cengage Learning, Inc.

Edit and Proofread

Grammar Workout: Check Participial Phrases

Use participial phrases to combine these sentences. Write the new sentence.

1. My goal is to be a reporter. I want to be covering the latest news.

_____

2. I know about Craig Kielburger's accomplishment. I asked him for an interview.

_____

3. Craig Kielburger's main focus is to help others. He founded a new organization.

_____

4. Free the Children is a humanitarian organization. This organization is dedicated to stopping child labor.

_____

Spelling Workout: Check Words with Greek and Latin Roots

Use the Greek and Latin roots in the chart to help you correct the spelling of the underlined words.

LATIN ROOT	MEANING
civis	city, citizenship
cogn	know
GREEK ROOT	**MEANING**
demo	people
phil	love for

Jim Kirk was never one for <u>sievics</u>, even though he is from

Philadelphia, the birthplace of American <u>demacracy</u>. He certainly was

no <u>filanthropist</u>. Then one day he met Edith Keeler, a civil-rights

attorney from Maryland. She made him <u>reckonize</u> the need to help

others. Now the two are married and spend their lives helping the less

fortunate.

Mechanics Workout: Check Commas

Add commas in each sentence as needed to set off participial phrases and appositives.

1. Disturbed by Masih's story Kielburger took the article to school.

2. He was inspired to begin his nonprofit organization Free the Children.

3. Dedicating itself to helping children around the world Free the Children raises money and awareness.

4. The people who are involved in Free the Children look up to Kielburger the founder of the organization.

5. More committed than ever Kielburger continues to work for the children of the world.

Check Grammar, Spelling, and Mechanics

Proofread the passage. Check the spelling of words with Greek and Latin roots, and the use of participial phrases. Check for commas that set off participial phrases and appositives. Correct the mistakes.

Editing and Proofreading Marks	
∧	Insert something.
⋏	Add a comma.
⋏	Add a semicolon.
⊙	Add a period.
⊙	Add a colon.
ᵛᵛ ᵛᵛ	Add quotation marks.
ᵛ	Add apostrophe.
≡	Capitalize.
╱	Make lower case.
℘	Delete.
¶	Make new paragraph.
◯	Check spelling.
⌢	Replace with this.
∼	Change order.
#	Insert space.
⌒	Close up.

Free the Children has been around since 1995. The organization has successfully removed many children from exploitive labor known around the world for its mission. Theirs is a filanthropic mission; they try to stay out of polotics as much as possible.

The organization has grown so large that other groups have come from it. A clothing company one dedicated to eco-friendly fabrics and methods has been started by the Kielburgers. Inspired by Free the Children this new company makes clothes in ways that don't harm people or the planet.

Edit and Proofread, continued

Edit and Proofread Your Essay

Now edit and proofread your work.

1. Use a checklist as you edit and proofread. Add things you are working on to the checklist.

2. Look to see which errors are marked most often. Jot down your top three trouble spots.

_____

_____

_____

3. Ask your teacher about ways to fix these mistakes, or check out the Grammar Handbook for information.

Focus on Spelling

Improve your spelling by following these steps.

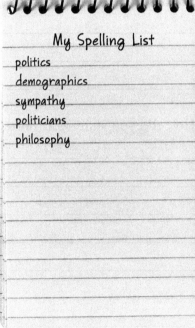

My Spelling List
politics
demographics
sympathy
politicians
philosophy

1. Create a personal spelling list. Record words that you misspelled. Look up correct spelling in the dictionary and add these words to **My Spelling List**.

2. Pick twelve words. Write each word four times. First write it in all lowercase letters. Next write it in all capital letters. After that, write the vowels in lowercase and the consonants in capitals. Last, write the word using fancy letters that you create on your own. For example, your letters can be curly, or tall and skinny.

3. Work with a partner to play **I'm Thinking of a Spelling Word.** Take turns giving each other clues. Some clues might be _I'm thinking of a word that rhymes with . . ., I'm thinking of a word that begins with . . ., or I'm thinking of a word that means . . ._ With each clue, the answer should include the word and its spelling.

4. Work with a partner to play a scrambled-letter game. Take each other's spelling words and write them in scrambled form. See which one of you can unscramble all the words first.

5. Use an audio recorder and record your words and their spelling. Then listen to your recording, checking to see that you spelled each word correctly.

Publish, Share, and Reflect

Publish and Share Your Cause-and-Effect Essay

Check the final formats you used to publish your cause-and-effect essay. Then answer the following questions.

1. Whether you published it by hand or on the computer, what did you do to dress up your final project?

_____

_____

_____

_____

_____

2. How did you share your work? What did you learn through sharing your work?

_____

_____

_____

_____

_____

_____

_____

_____

_____

_____

_____

_____

Publish, Share, and Reflect, continued

Reflect on Your Cause-and-Effect Essay

Read your cause-and-effect essay. Then answer questions 1–6.

1. What do you like best about your work? _____

_____

_____

2. What did you do well? _____

_____

_____

3. What could you improve about your work? _____

_____

_____

_____

4. Is your writing clear and focused? _____

_____

_____

5. Did writing about cause and effects help you understand your topic better? What did you learn from writing this essay? _____

_____

_____

_____

6. Will you add your cause-and-effect essay to your Writing Portfolio? Explain your decision.

❏ Yes, I will add this to my Writing Portfolio.

_____

_____

❏ No, I will not add this to my Writing Portfolio.

_____

_____

Analyze a Public Service Announcement

What makes a good public service announcement?
Read the passages and answer the questions.

Passage 1

The Food Pyramid

People should use the food pyramid to plan healthy meals. The U.S. Department of Agriculture created a food guide pyramid. It shows what foods are in each food group. It also shows how much of each food you need to eat each day for a healthy diet. The pyramid includes grains and vegetables. It also shows fruits, dairy, and meats and proteins.

Passage 2

Say Yes to a Healthy Diet

Would you like to say no to that extra cookie or slice of apple pie? You should use the food guide pyramid issued by the U.S. Department of Agriculture (USDA) to plan healthy meals. According to the USDA, the largest part of our daily diet should come from fruits, vegetables, dairy, and grains—preferably whole grains. Smaller portions of meats, proteins, fats, and oils round out a healthy diet. Once you understand the food pyramid, you will be more likely to make healthy food choices.

1. Compare the two passages. Which passage captures your interest? How?

_____

_____

_____

_____

_____

_____

2. What position do the writers of both passages take?

_____

_____

_____

_____

_____

_____

3. Which passage provides better support for the position? Explain.

_____

_____

_____

_____

_____

_____

Write Effective Sentences

Vary Your Sentences

Rewrite the following paragraph using the Recipe for Sentence Variety.

More farms should convert to organic farming. I live on an organic farm. In order for our farm to be "organic," we had to get certification. To get certification, we had to prove that we don't use synthetic fertilizers, chemical pesticides, or sewage sludge. Our farm had to be chemical-free for more than three years. We also had to make sure we kept all of the organic products away from any non-organic items. It has taken a lot of work. We are happy that we "went organic."

_____

_____

_____

_____

_____

_____

_____

_____

_____

_____

_____

_____

_____

_____

_____

_____

_____

Streamline Your Sentences

Rewrite the paragraph to make the sentences more streamlined.

Ways to Streamline Sentences
- cut down wordiness
- combine sentences with appositives.

Saturday is the best day of the week. I love Saturdays. Each and every Saturday, my mom, dad, brother, and I get up. We drive to the farmers' market in our town. A large number of people come to the farmers' market each week. We start our day at a bakery. It is called "Rolling in Dough." My brother always orders the same thing for breakfast. He orders a fresh apple fritter. I like trying something new every week. Then I decide if I like it. The owner suggests one of her weekly specials. Then I try it. After breakfast is over, we shop for our favorite fruits, vegetables, bread, fish, and meat for the rest of the week. Then we'll do it all again next Saturday!

© National Geographic Learning, a part of Cengage Learning, Inc.

Write Effective Sentences, continued

Keep Your Sentences Parallel

Rewrite the paragraph to make the sentences parallel.

> People need safer drinking water. Some water is not safe to drink. That's because it's full of chemicals, pesticides, and is polluted. It makes more sense for people to drink bottled water than risking drinking dirty water. Dirty water tastes bad, looks ugly, and people can get sick from it. Something that is washed in dirty water, like fruits, vegetables, or meats that are raw, can become dirty. Many people do not know that eating food washed in dirty water can harm them. People must also be careful when playing, boating, or as they swim in dirty water.

Plan a Public Service Announcement

Use pages 202–203 to plan your public service announcement.

1. Write down some issues you feel strongly about, either for or against.

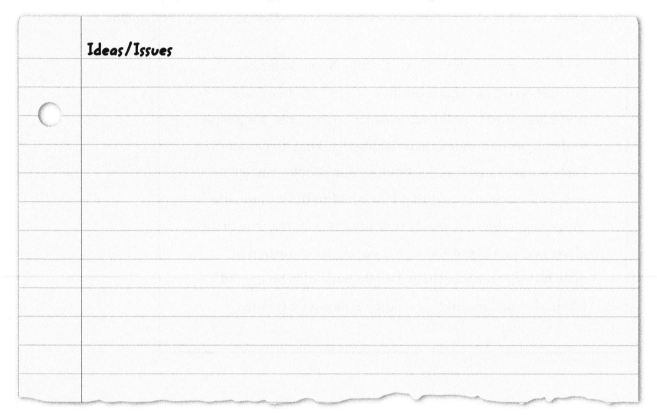

Ideas/Issues

2. Pick your three best ideas or issues. List the good and bad points of each. Then circle the issue that you want to write about.

Ideas/Issues	Good and Bad Points

Plan a Public Service Announcement, continued

3. Write your opener. Include an attention-getting first sentence and a clear statement of your position.

_____

_____

_____

_____

_____

_____

4. Organize your support. List your evidence in order of strength. Then write an objection to it and a counterclaim or rebuttal.

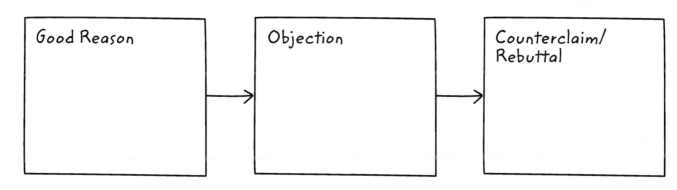

Good Reason	Objection	Counterclaim/ Rebuttal

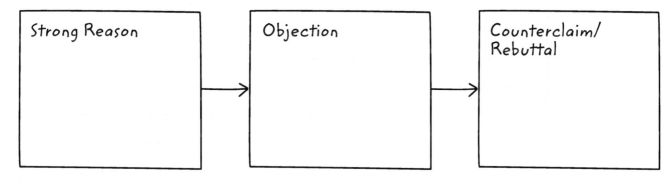

Strong Reason	Objection	Counterclaim/ Rebuttal

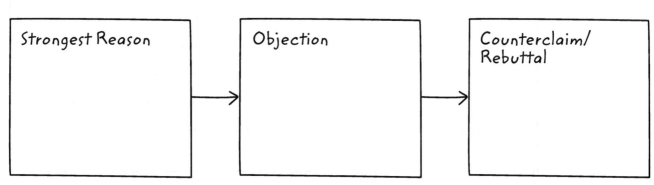

Strongest Reason	Objection	Counterclaim/ Rebuttal

Level C
Project 15: Write as an Advocate

Writing Application: Prewrite

Draft a Public Service Announcement

Use your plan from pages 202–203 to write the first draft of your public service announcement.

Drafting Checklist

- [ ] Capture the listeners' interest.
- [ ] Clearly state your position.
- [ ] Distinguish your position from opposing views.
- [ ] Support your position with logical reasons and relevant evidence.
- [ ] Use transition words to connect your ideas.
- [ ] Use a formal tone throughout.
- [ ] Conclude with a statement that follows from your argument.

Draft a Public Service Announcement, continued

Revise a Public Service Announcement

1. Use the checklist to evaluate this draft of a public service announcement. What changes are needed?

_____

_____

_____

_____

_____

_____

_____

_____

Revising Checklist

☐ Do you capture the listeners' interest?

☐ Do you clearly state your position?

☐ Do you distinguish your position from opposing views?

☐ Do you support your position with logical reasons and relevant evidence?

☐ Do you use a formal tone throughout?

☐ Do you conclude with a statement that follows from your argument?

2. Revise the draft. Use revising marks to show your changes.

Revising

MARK	WHAT IT MEANS
∧	Insert something.
↶	Move to here.
∧—	Replace with this.
⌐	Take out.
¶	Make a new paragraph.

The Most Important Meal of the Day

According to nutritionists, breakfast is the most important meal of the day, and you should not skip it. Many students feel that they get more from getting the extra sleep in the morning, but skipping breakfast can have a bad effect on the rest of your day. Some students rely on cafeteria breakfasts, which may not always be available. If you skip breakfast, you're going to eat more for lunch. Eating more at lunch will have a negative effect on your body over time. You should get up earlier to be sure you have time to eat breakfast.

3. Now use the checklist to help you revise the draft of your public service announcement on pages 204–205. Use a clean sheet of paper.

Edit and Proofread

Grammar Workout: Check Present Perfect Tense

Complete each sentence with the present perfect tense of the verb in parentheses.

1. For the past two summers, Gus and I _____ at the Food Bank.
(volunteer)

2. We _____ to do something for others for a long time.
(want)

3. Gus _____ the responsibility for organizing all the canned goods.
(take)

4. He _____ them by fruits, vegetables, and soups.
(arrange)

5. I _____ the rest of the shelves with packages of rice and noodles.
(fill)

Spelling Workout: Check Words with -y

Read each sentence. Use proofreading marks to correct the spelling errors.

1. Mr. Reese knows how to fix satisfing meals.

2. A retired chef, he fixes the healthyiest meals I've ever tasted.

3. One day, I told him about people at the soup kitchen who tryed to feed everyone.

4. "Everyone enjoys the tiny amount they get," they said. "But we wish there was more."

5. That very day, Mr. Reese carryied a giant pot of his homemade stew there!

Mechanics Workout: Check Commas, Ellipses, and Dashes

Read each sentence. Use editing marks to add commas, dashes, or ellipses where they belong.

1. Sometimes I wish it were different you have to fight for what's right.

2. My dad went to the community meeting rally and pot-luck to support a new shelter.

3. He feels so does Mom that it's important to help others.

4. Where would we get housing if?

5. Voting for the new shelter Dad and Mom are doing their part.

Check Grammar, Spelling, and Mechanics

Proofread the passage. Check the spelling, the use of present perfect tense verbs, and the use of punctuation to show breaks and pauses. Correct the mistakes.

Editing and Proofreading Marks	
∧	Insert something.
⩘	Add a comma.
⩙	Add a semicolon.
⊙	Add a period.
⊙	Add a colon.
⩔ ⩔	Add quotation marks.
⩔	Add apostrophe.
≡	Capitalize.
/	Make lower case.
⸎	Delete.
¶	Make new paragraph.
◯	Check spelling.
⌒	Replace with this.
∼	Change order.
#	Insert space.
◡	Close up.

My grandma have lived with us happily for several years. But the last few days she has seemed sad bored and cranky. I was worryied about her until my neighbor mentioned the Senior Center down the street. "There," he said, "many older adults has maked new friends and have finded activityes they enjoy. Staiing active is important for everyone, including older adults." Willing to try it Grandma went to the center the next day, the day after that,

Now Grandma believe it or not is the happyest she's ever been!

© National Geographic Learning, a part of Cengage Learning, Inc.

Edit and Proofread, continued

Edit and Proofread Your Public Service Announcement

Now edit and proofread your work.

1. Use a checklist as you edit and proofread. Add things you are working on to the checklist.

2. Look to see which errors are marked most often. Jot down your top three trouble spots.

_____

_____

_____

3. Ask your teacher about ways to fix these mistakes, or check out the Grammar Handbook for information.

Focus on Spelling

Improve your spelling by following these steps.

1. Create a personal spelling list. Record words that you misspelled. Look up correct spelling in the dictionary and add these words to **My Spelling List**.

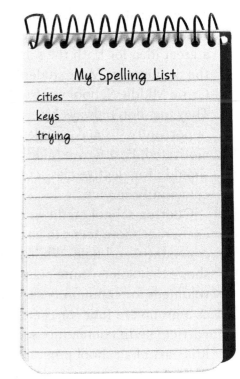

My Spelling List
cities
keys
trying

2. Pick twelve words. Make each word look interesting and special by tracing it five times. Write the word in one color. Then trace it four times in four different colors. Say each letter to yourself as you trace it.

3. Work with a partner to play **Spelling Catch**. Pitch words to each other by saying "Here's the windup. Here's the pitch. The word is . . ." Take turns pitching. The first "batter" to spell ten words correctly wins.

4. Play a scrambled-letter game with a partner. Take each other's spelling words and write them in scrambled forms. See who can unscramble all the words first.

5. Use an audio recorder and record your words and their spelling. Then listen to your recording, checking to see that you spelled each word correctly.

Analyze a Persuasive Essay

What makes this persuasive essay a good model?
Read the essay and answer the questions.

Let's Factor In Community-Service Credit

by Alan Javitz

It's not that hard to help others. Simple tasks, such as holding the door for someone or carrying an elderly person's groceries, can be a big help to others. Students can often be some of the most helpful people in their communities. In fact, more and more schools across the country are requiring students to perform community service. However, many students just don't take time to help.

Community-service credit hours are a great idea for both the school and the community. Most students at East Grove Middle School want to help. They just don't always have the time or opportunity. To make students more motivated, East Grove Middle School should give elective class credits for community service.

Offering school credit will encourage more teens to go into the community and help. While research shows that some young people volunteer for community service, teens as a group are four times more likely to participate in community service when it is part of a school program. In fact, 93% of teens from schools offering elective credits for community service participated in at least one activity. In contrast, 24% of those from schools without such programs chose to go out and help on their own. Course credit will make community service not only available, but desirable as well.

Feature Checklist

A good persuasive essay

☐ states the writer's position on the issue

☐ appeals to logic using evidence

☐ appeals to emotions using persuasive language

☐ addresses the opposing argument

☐ ends with a call to action.

1. What is the writer's position on the issue?

_____

_____

_____

_____

_____

_____

2. What reasons does the writer give to support his position?

_____

_____

_____

_____

_____

_____

3. What evidence does the writer use to make a logical appeal?

_____

_____

_____

_____

_____

_____

© National Geographic Learning, a part of Cengage Learning, Inc.

Analyze a Persuasive Essay, continued

Some people may argue that encouraging students to participate in community service during school hours takes them away from their "important" classes. However, giving students class credit for community service will actually help them become better students. Reports show that students involved in community service perform better in school. They also develop new career goals and learn about career options. Helping in the community motivates students to keep learning. It inspires some students to prepare for jobs in the public sector. When teens are given the opportunity to make a difference, it builds their self-esteem. They find the confidence they need to succeed in other areas of their lives.

Teens involved in community service also become better citizens. They are able to connect to people they may never have met otherwise. They also have opportunities to develop leadership skills, learn to respect others, and understand how to be good citizens. After all, isn't learning to help others as important as doing class work?

The research is undeniable: offering teens the opportunity, and the incentive, to perform community service is good for everyone. I urge the leaders at East Grove Middle School to offer class credit for community-service hours.

4. How does the writer address the opposing argument?

_____

_____

_____

_____

_____

_____

5. How does the writer make an emotional appeal?

_____

_____

_____

_____

_____

6. How does the essay end?

_____

_____

_____

_____

_____

_____

_____

_____

Appeal to Logic

Read the paragraph. Then rewrite it to include appeals to logic.
Use information from the Evidence Bank to support your argument.

Collecting for the Hungry

Many people in the United States live with hunger daily. There are also people in the United States who have no place to live. Canned-food drives are a great way to help end the hunger problem in our nation. Food banks often have trouble keeping food on the shelves, and food drives can help. If done correctly, a canned-food drive can collect a lot of food for the hungry. Many people waste food that they buy from the supermarket. Why not donate that food to a canned-food drive instead?

Evidence Bank

- Food drives allow food banks to provide a wide variety of nutritious foods throughout the year.

- According to a 2006 study, there were 35.5 million hungry people in the United States.

- One food drive collected 1,229 pounds of food, which was enough for 960 meals.

- Many households throw away 10% of food they buy at the supermarket, which equals about 470 pounds.

- A 2005 study found that there were 744,313 homeless people in the United States.

- Canned foods are ideal because they last for a long time on shelves and are easy to transport and distribute.

_____

_____

_____

_____

_____

_____

_____

_____

_____

_____

_____

_____

Appeal to Emotion

Read the paragraph. Then rewrite it to include appeals to emotion. Use persuasive language and personal examples (make one up if you need to!) to support your argument.

Donating Food

Donating food to a food drive is one thing people can do to help the hungry. Many people have food stocked in their pantry. Food drives welcome all donations. The only rule is that the food must not be expired. A few cans of food will provide a lot of meals for the hungry. You can collect cans from your neighbors or start a food drive at your school. You might be surprised by all the people who are willing to help. Giving food to a food drive will help improve others' lives.

_____

_____

_____

_____

_____

_____

_____

_____

_____

_____

_____

_____

_____

_____

_____

_____

_____

_____

Support Your Arguments

This persuasive essay could be more effective. Read the essay.
Then revise it by adding

- supporting facts (You may need to do a little research.)
- details to clarify and elaborate
- persuasive language to convince the reader.

More Calcium for Better Bones

Did you know that a lot of boys and girls aged 9–18 fail to get the recommended amount of calcium? Not getting enough calcium in your diet can lead to problems. Calcium is the building block for strong bones. Because your bones continue to grow into your teens, it is important to supply them with the proper nutrients. There are many ways to get more calcium in your diet.

One way is directly from the foods that you eat. There are a lot of foods that naturally contain calcium. You can also look for foods that are fortified with calcium. Fortified foods are a good way for people who have dairy allergies to get calcium.

As growing teenagers, you should be more aware of how much calcium you consume. Taking small steps can help you achieve a large percentage of your daily recommended calcium intake. So next time you pack your lunch or pick up a snack at the school cafeteria, think about what you are eating. Look for foods that contain dairy products, or check the nutrition information to see if it is fortified with calcium.

© National Geographic Learning, a part of Cengage Learning, Inc.

Use Charts, Tables, and Pictures

Read each argument. Consider the graphics that could support it. Then circle the letter of the graphic that you think would best support the argument. Explain your choice.

1. Because there are more homeless people now than in past years, we should increase the frequency of canned-food drives to one a month.

A. a photo of a group of homeless persons

B. a pie chart showing the types of canned foods that homeless persons prefer

C. a graph showing how the number of homeless people has increased over a span of 10 years

_____

_____

_____

_____

_____

_____

2. Our school should plan field trips to feed the homeless. More students favor field trips than running canned-food drives and collecting donations.

A. a photo of students riding on a bus to a local homeless shelter

B. a table showing the cost of field trips to five different homeless shelters around the city

C. a pie chart showing the percentage of students who support field trips to feed the homeless and the percentage of students who prefer other options

_____

_____

_____

_____

_____

_____

3. Our school should provide healthier food choices in the cafeteria. This will increase participation in after-school sports.

    A. a graph showing how the number of healthy food choices has increased in city schools

    B. a table showing participation in after-school sports at schools with healthy food choices and without healthy food choices

    C. a photo of healthy food choices offered in cafeterias across the country

_____

_____

_____

_____

_____

_____

4. Color-coded stickers would be more effective than lists of ingredients in helping students choose healthy snacks in the cafeteria. Green would mean "healthy"; yellow would mean "okay"; red would mean "avoid."

    A. photos showing foods with colored stickers and foods with lists of ingredients that are hard to read

    B. a table comparing the number of unhealthy snack foods sold in cafeterias around the county

    C. a pie chart showing the proportion of students who have said they would like guidance in choosing healthy snacks

_____

_____

_____

_____

_____

_____

Plan a Persuasive Essay

Use pages 217–218 to plan your persuasive essay.

1. Choose an issue and a position. Jot down some food issues that affect you or your community. Explain your position on each issue and what you want people to do about it.

Issues I Care About

_____

_____

_____

_____

_____

_____

_____

_____

_____

_____

2. Gather evidence to support your position. Write down the arguments you want to make in your essay. Then record evidence that supports each argument.

Argument	Evidence

3. Organize your main supporting points. Use the graphic organizer to identify your main position and your supporting arguments.

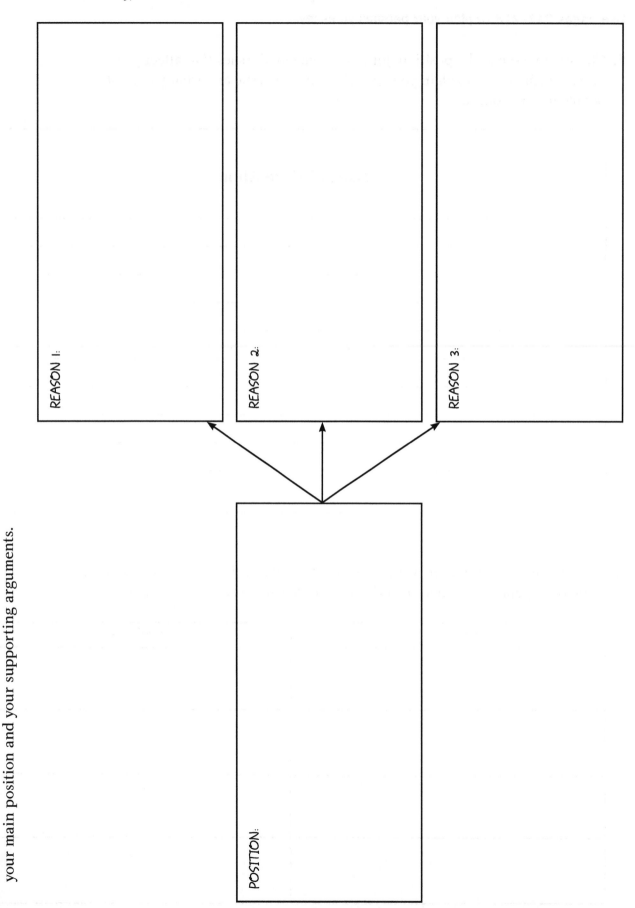

REASON 1:

REASON 2:

REASON 3:

POSITION:

Draft a Persuasive Essay

Use your plan from pages 217–218 to write the first draft
of your persuasive essay.

Drafting Checklist

- ☐ State your position in the introduction.
- ☐ Give background and reasons to support your position.
- ☐ Appeal to logic using evidence.
- ☐ Appeal to emotions using persuasive language.
- ☐ Strengthen your argument with charts, tables, and pictures.
- ☐ End with a call to action in the conclusion.

Revise a Persuasive Essay

1. Use the checklist to evaluate this draft of a persuasive essay. What changes are needed?

_____

_____

_____

_____

_____

_____

Revising Checklist

☐ Do you need to add examples or details to support your position?

☐ Can you make your word choice more precise and interesting?

☐ Can you streamline wordy or repetitive sentences?

☐ Can you combine any sentences to make your writing more sophisticated?

2. Revise this draft. Use revising marks to show your changes.

Revising

MARK	WHAT IT MEANS
∧	Insert something.
↶	Move to here.
∧	Replace with this.
⸜	Take out.
¶	Make a new paragraph.

Volunteerism

We all want to live in an ideal world. But few of us want to help create that world. It is up to us to make the world a better place. One of the best ways to do that is by volunteering. Volunteering can be difficult, but it is rewarding work.

There are many ways to volunteer, so it is best to choose something that you like. You can help at homeless shelters, clean up parks, or assist at senior centers. There are hundreds of things you can do. Every little bit helps make our world a better place, both for us and the future.

3. Now use the checklist to help you revise the draft of your persuasive essay on pages 219–220.

Edit and Proofread

Grammar Workout: Check Verb Consistency

Rewrite each sentence. Make the voice and mood of the verbs consistent.

1. Last week, we read an article about obesity and would learn how it is a big problem in this country.

_____

_____

2. I already knew a lot about the subject. The problem was researched by my partner and me before.

_____

_____

3. We worried about the problem and listed some solutions. The issue is taken seriously by us.

_____

_____

4. If we don't do something about obesity now, make it worse in the future.

_____

_____

Spelling Workout:
Check Words with _q_, _ie_, and _ei_

Read each sentence. Use proofreading marks to correct the spelling errors.

1. I've reduced my eating portions by a qarter so that I will be healthier.

2. I've even started eating vegetables, which is a big releif to my mother.

3. Other kids in my nieghborhood have started doing the same thing.

4. I've also concieved a plan that will help other students eat better.

5. I plan to ask our principal to qit serving junk food in the cafeteria.

Name _____ Date _____

Edit and Proofread, continued

Mechanics Workout: Check Capitalization of Proper Adjectives and Academic Courses

Use revising marks to fix the capitalization in the sentences below.

1. In my Science Class, we are learning about the effects of unhealthy eating.

2. Because the american population is eating too much, people are having problems.

3. Low-fat chinese and japanese foods can be healthy alternatives.

4. My sister, who is taking introduction to nutrition in college, is telling me what to eat.

Check Grammar, Spelling, and Mechanics

Proofread the passage. Check the spelling, the capitalization of proper adjectives and academic courses, and consistent verb tense, voice, and mood. Correct the mistakes.

Editing and Proofreading Marks	
∧	Insert something.
⋏	Add a comma.
⋏	Add a semicolon.
⊙	Add a period.
⊙	Add a colon.
ᕁ ᕁ	Add quotation marks.
ᕁ	Add an apostrophe.
≡	Capitalize.
/	Make lowercase.
℘	Delete.
¶	Make new paragraph.
◯	Check spelling.
⌒	Replace with this.
∽	Change order.
#	Insert space.
⌣	Close up.

I am writing an essay about cafeteria foods. It was assigned by my science teacher. The essay was easy because I had done this last year for my know your body class. I am concerned about the american obesity crisis and our school's contribution to it. In the cafeteria, candy bars and sodas are sold. I beleive that these foods qalify as junk food. I want our school to stop selling these foods. If the foods are not available for students to eat, then they don't be tempted. I also think we should have some Vegetarian entrees, such as indian, chinese, and japanese dishes. Last week I began a petition. By tomorrow, I recieved 200 signatures. I hope the principal will listen to me now.

Level C
Project 16: Write as a Citizen

223

Writing Application: Edit and Proofread

Edit and Proofread Your Persuasive Essay

Now edit and proofread your work.

Remember to Check

- ☐ consistency of verb voice and mood
- ☐ words with *q*, *ie*, and *ei*
- ☐ capitalization of proper adjectives and academic courses
- ☐ _____
- ☐ _____

1. Use a checklist as you edit and proofread. Add things you are working on to the checklist.

2. Look to see which errors are marked most often. Jot down your top three trouble spots.

_____

_____

_____

3. Ask your teacher about ways to fix these mistakes, or check out the Grammar Handbook for information.

Focus on Spelling

Improve your spelling by following these steps.

1. Create a personal spelling list. Record words that you misspelled. Look up correct spelling in the dictionary and add these words to **My Spelling List**.

2. Pick twelve words. Make each word look interesting and special by tracing it five times. Write the word in one color. Then trace it four times in four different colors. Say each letter to yourself as you trace it.

3. Work with a partner to play **Spelling Catch**. Pitch words to each other by saying "Here's the windup. Here's the pitch. The word is . . ." Take turns pitching. The first "batter" to spell ten words correctly wins.

My Spelling List

quest
Qatar
achieve
friend
weigh

4. Write each spelling word. Then write it again and circle all the consonants. Write it one more time and circle all the vowels.

5. Play **Memory** to help you remember your words. Write each spelling word on two different index cards and place them face down. Turn the cards over two at a time. Your goal is to find the matching cards. Say and spell the words on the cards as you turn them over. If you make a match, remove those cards from the game. You've won when you've removed all the cards.

Publish, Share, and Reflect

Publish and Share Your Persuasive Essay

**Check the final formats you used to publish your persuasive essay.
Then answer the following questions.**

Publishing

What was the final format of your project?	How did you share your project?
☐ Wrote it neatly by hand	☐ Shared it with a large group
☐ Typed it on a computer	☐ Shared it with a small group

1. Whether you published it by hand or on the computer, what did you do to dress up your final project?

_____

_____

_____

_____

_____

2. How did you share your work? What did you learn through sharing your work?

_____

_____

_____

_____

_____

_____

_____

_____

_____

_____

_____

_____

_____

_____

Reflect on Your Persuasive Essay

Read your persuasive essay. Then answer questions 1–6.

1. What do you like best about your work? _____

_____

_____

2. What did you do well? _____

_____

_____

3. What could you improve about your work? _____

_____

_____

_____

4. What did you learn about this issue from writing about it? _____

_____

_____

5. Has your position on this issue changed at all? _____

_____

_____

6. Will you add your persuasive essay to your Writing Portfolio? Explain your decision.

☐ Yes, I will add this to my Writing Portfolio.

_____

_____

☐ No, I will not add this to my Writing Portfolio.

_____

_____